"SO WHAT IF I'M 50?"

Other Books by Bob Weinstein

RÉSUMÉS DON'T GET JOBS: THE REALITIES AND MYTHS OF JOB HUNTING

"I'LL WORK FOR FREE"

JOBS FOR THE 21ST CENTURY

HOW TO SWITCH CAREERS

HOW TO GET A JOB IN HARD TIMES

"SO WHAT IF I'M 50?"

Straight Talk and Proven Strategies
for Getting Hired in the
Toughest Job Market Ever

BOB WEINSTEIN

McGraw-Hill

New York   San Francisco   Washington, D.C.   Auckland   Bogotá
Caracas   Lisbon   London   Madrid   Mexico City   Milan
Montreal   New Delhi   San Juan   Singapore
Sydney   Tokyo   Toronto

Library of Congress Cataloging-in-Publication Data

Weinstein, Bob, date.
    So what if I'm 50? : straight talk and proven strategies for
getting hired in the toughest job market ever / Bob Weinstein.
        p.   cm.
    Includes index.
    ISBN 0-07-069189-4 (pbk.)
    1. Job hunting.   2. Middle aged persons—Employment.   I. Title.
HF5382.7.W444   1996
650.14′084′4—dc20   95-41687
                                                          CIP

McGraw-Hill

A Division of The McGraw-Hill Companies

1 2 3 4 5 6 7 8 9 0   QBP/QBP   9 0 0 9 8 7 6 5

ISBN 0-07-069189-4

*The sponsoring editor for this book was Betsy Brown, the editing
supervisor was Fred Bernardi, and the production supervisor was
Pamela Pelton. It was set in Fairfield by Teresa F. Leaden of McGraw-
Hill's Professional Book Group composition unit.*

Printed and bound by Quebecor-Book Press

McGraw-Hill books are available at special quantity discounts to
use as premiums and sales promotions, or for use in corporate
training programs. For more information, please write to the
Director of Special Sales, McGraw-Hill, 11 West 19th Street, New
York, NY 10011. Or contact your local bookstore.

For Bonnie

CONTENTS

ACKNOWLEDGMENTS

This book was a labor of love from start to finish. The project would not have been successful if it weren't for the countless sources who willingly participated. More than a job-hunting manual for 50-plus job hunters, they realized I was setting the record straight by joyfully telling older workers they were not *just* as competent as their younger counterparts, they were *better*. I appreciate the help and support of the countless agencies, private and nonprofit, that showered me with information and statistics. Once again, special thanks to my friend and colleague Tom Popp for helping me whip the manuscript into shape; my son-in-law Enrique Ball for being my *Boston Globe* clipping service; my wife, Bonnie, for putting up with a lunatic journalist all these years; my children, Jenny and Josh, for being my greatest supporters; and last, T. "Pete" Bonner, my blast-from-the-past high school buddy for hanging out with me all these years.

Bob Weinstein

"SO WHAT IF I'M 50?"

WHO YOU CALLING OLD?

Age 50 is the great divide. Hit the big 5-0 and suddenly you're labeled as old. The common perception is you've slowed to a crawl. Your card has been punched. Time is running out fast. You're on the last lap. Suddenly, you've been thrust into a strange world with its own terminology. As you wend your way toward 60, you'll take on a new identity and status. You're soon to join the ranks of senior citizens. Why not call them "chronologically challenged"? All the cosmetic surgery in the world isn't going to change things.

With advanced age comes special treatment. Some people call it respect, but activist groups call it second-class citizenship, not to mention prejudice. And there is no reason for it.

Flail all you want about this injustice, but get used to the fact that things aren't going to change so fast. Today's culture is obsessed with youth—looking and acting young. As you get older, you're ostracized and treated badly. The very people you coached, tutored, and nurtured suddenly give you the cold shoulder. It seems like just yesterday you gave them jobs and helped them build careers. Now the tables have turned. They don't want to know you, because you're perceived as stale and used up. To build a business, fresh blood—not tired old platelets supercharged with Geritol—is needed.

A NEW SET OF RULES

Get with the program. *Different rules* apply to older workers. Cross the 65 barrier and you can take advantage of reduced train, bus, and plane fares and get into movies and theaters at hefty discounts. There are also umpteen travel packages to all parts of the globe.

Bargains are great, but the related innuendos are repugnant. No longer part of the mainstream, you're relegated to a different category; you're part of a select club you never intended to join.

Many third-world countries and the entire continent of Asia venerate their elders. We ship ours out to retirement communities and nursing homes. Terrified and obsessed with our own mortality, we ostracize rather than enfold our elders. One day we're part of the action, the next we're has-beens watching life on the six o'clock news. Maggie Kuhn, founder of special-interest group the Gray Panthers, compared society's treatment of the elderly to tossing old cars in a junkyard. Said Kuhn: "The junkyard haunts me because America does the same thing to people." When we turn 55, we're trashed. Acknowledging that age does, in some ways, determine what people are capable of, the Gray Panthers insist that a distinction be drawn between the effects of aging and assumptions about those effects—assumptions based on ill-founded stereotypes (see Chap. Three).

No wonder older workers are having a tough time finding work. The sad part is that many actually believe they're over the hill. Why not sound the death knell? Like Skinner's rats, we've been conditioned by slick marketing and advertising programs that have stratified the marketplace into age, income, and demographic categories.

Get the picture? The problem is we're letting others call the shots. We've been brainwashed. Current thinking dictates old is bad, young is good. An article in *The New York Times* summed up this attitude. The headline read "Age, Beauty, and Truth," followed by subline "Marketers are proclaiming that older women are beautiful." Fantastic. Just what women have been waiting for—the stamp of approval. But don't get excited. The world isn't changing. It's just corporate America hitting you up for money. Clinique, the youth-oriented division of Estee Lauder Inc., is peddling its wares to women over 50 because their demographics translate into dollars.

Ken Dykewald, a gerontologist, formed Age Wave, a consulting and marketing company in Emeryville, CA, that advises corporations on how to cash in on older clientele. He says the 50-plus generation will grow by 12 million in the 1990s. What's more, in this decade alone they're going to have more than $300 billion in spending power. And they're recession-proof. That spells power in any language.

Suffice it to say Americans have a serious problem with aging. The over-50 crowd could use some good public relations. The pity is *we* don't need it. Yes, I'm 50 and proud of it.

I don't have to tell you this is the most competitive job market ever. The downsizing of America, which began in the mid-1980s, will continue through the 1990s. The proverbial bottom line is, good jobs are hard to find. For the over-50, it's twice as hard.

THE AMERICAN DREAM IS STILL UP FOR GRABS

That's the battlefield you face. But I'm going to show you how to win. This book is not only going to get you working; it's going to give you a new take on life. Uppermost, you'll stop apologizing for your age. You'll tell smart-ass kids who think anyone over 50 ought to be checking out cemetery plots to take another look. In a few decades, they'll be there too and I guarantee they won't look as good as you do.

The task at hand is first learning how to turn around your life. Then it's mastering the fine art of negotiation to get what you want. The idea is to work till you drop and hang around people who appreciate and respect your experience, knowledge, reliability, and maturity.

Before you don your Sunday finest and pound the pavement searching for jobs, overhaul your attitude and get tough. Even though the ground rules are different, don't let anyone tell you there are no job openings. There are plenty, if you know where to look.

The bad news is deeply ingrained prejudices against older workers are not going to disappear overnight—if ever.

Don't let that stop you. The good news is opportunities are created by the very machinery that put you on the street. Job permanence is a thing of the past; job hopping is the leitmotif for the future. Employers are looking, not for lifetime employees, but for talented, motivated employees who'll work for 5 to 8 years. That spells opportunity in billboard-size letters for older workers.

Let's find out how the new career world works. The first step is turning 50-year-old heads around. Face it. Job searchers over 50 are depressed for good reason. Hell, we're only human. What can we expect after digesting decades of negative programming? We've been brainwashed into thinking we don't stand a chance against younger workers. This attitude is so ingrained that many of us crawl through the day thinking we're second-class citizens, runners-up to confident 33-year-olds. No wonder thousands have thrown in the towel. I'll show you there is a big exciting world out there waiting to be savored. But you're going to have to jump into the ring to grab a piece. Trust me, you're more in shape than you realize. The real reason is *you deserve it.*

This book is about doing the work you love for as long as you want. I'm going to help you determine the kinds of jobs you want and then show you how to find them. I'm also going to tell you about some interesting options you've never considered.

Uppermost, I promise straight talk from a guy who's been there. I spent over 20 years in the corporate arena working for others. I know how the game is played. More important, I know what it takes to win.

Let's get started.

GET OVER YOURSELF

"Sorry, you don't have the qualifications we're looking for." Every day across America, older workers swallow a line like this from employers. And it's always delivered by a smiling, perky human resources person 20 years their junior.

What employers actually mean, but can't say because of a possible age bias lawsuit, is "Your qualifications are great, but you're too old. We want someone younger for this job." In short, you're over the hill.

Sound familiar? Before I discuss the solutions and strategies, let's look at the obstacles and competition you're up against. Attitudes toward older workers haven't changed much over the past century. In fact, many experts insist they've gotten worse—thanks to a fiercely competitive economy beset by rampant downsizing.

STRENGTH IN NUMBERS

The good news is you're not alone. In fact, your ranks are increasing dramatically. After rising less than 3 percent between 1979 and 1992, the number of U.S. workers 55 and older will increase 38 percent by 2005—more than either African-Americans or women, according to the U.S. Department of Labor. By the year 2025, when baby boomers reach old age, more than 20 percent of the population will be over 65.

Yet in the shadow of a swelling army of older workers, age discrimination is alive and thriving. It doesn't matter that it's illegal, according to Equal Employment Opportunity Commission (EEOC) laws. The many national studies that have driven this point home are little consolation to a qualified person pushing 50 who loses a job to someone less qualified and 20 years his or her junior.

A recent national study conducted by the American Association of Retired Persons (AARP) found that in cases where two fictional people, ages 57 and 32, mailed practically identical résumés to 775 large companies, the companies discriminated 26.5 percent of the time against the older worker. Exec-U-Net, an executive networking service in Norwalk, CT, surveyed its 2000 members and found that age discrimination begins as early as 40. After 50, executives secured only 45 percent as many interviews as the 35–39 set. Those 45–49 received only 47 percent as many interviews as those 35–39.

It's no wonder age-bias suits have surged 14 percent in the last 2 years. The prejudice against older workers is so ingrained it defies logic. Employers have yet to understand that no correlation exists between age and ability. But it goes far deeper than that.

AT WAR WITH YUPPIES

If you're looking for justice, forget it. It doesn't exist. Wake up and smell the coffee. Here's a true story to match the cliché.

Ever wonder why practically all the specialty "coffee bars" have twentyish types mixing those foaming cappuccinos and lattes for a growing legion of consumers addicted to gourmet coffee? When is the last time you saw a fiftyish or, perish the thought, sixtyish person working there?

A 53-year-old out-of-work actor friend rejected for a manager's job at two of New York's trendiest coffee chains discovered why. It's not that he wasn't qualified. He's managed posh New York eateries and logged in a decade and a half as a waiter. He looks pretty good too, even though his hair is graying and a mite thin at the top. Yet he didn't look good enough to cut the hip yuppie image these coffee purveyors try to project.

After hearing his story, I checked out Starbucks, Seattle Coffee Roasters, and a couple of other cool New York coffee hangouts. Not a fiftyish-looking person in the place. Starbucks, for one, is expanding rapidly, with new locations all over the country. A call to its regional employment office in Washington, DC, revealed its hiring parameters. The taped message said, "Apply in person to the store nearest you" for sales jobs paying $6.30 an hour. For management slots, mail your résumé to the company and it will get back to you if interested.

Granted, the pay is nothing to get excited about, yet plenty of 50-year-olds would take these jobs while waiting for something more substantial to materialize. It beats slinging burgers in McDonald's.

Similarly, show your face for a sales job and you're doomed. You'll be lucky if you capture an interview after sending in your résumé. They'll see a string of impressive positions and stamp you "overqualified" and too old for the trendy look they're marketing.

The answer is, older workers are bad for their image. Try to prove that in court.

One more true story. A 55-year-old woman in the midst of a career change tried to secure a slot in the training program of one of Los Angeles' top talent agencies. Wanna-be agents practically kill to secure a job with this firm, whose clients include a list of superstar actors, writers, filmmakers, and producers. Outgoing, warm, attractive, and smart, the woman had the right ingredients for the job. Yet it didn't take an Einstein to figure out she was over 45. You guessed it. She was rejected, given the obligatory lame excuse she wasn't qualified. Meanwhile, this high-profile firm boasts an egalitarian hiring philosophy, a reputation of hiring lawyers and accountants, even computer programmers, who have what it deems "outgoing and dynamic personality traits" for the high-profile job.

You get the picture. Thousands of other examples can be cited. Jack Levin, a sociology professor at Northeastern University in Boston, says the interests of elders and youths have been pitted against each other. Some fanatical ultraconservative interest groups argue that the status of the elderly has greatly improved at the expense of the well-being of the young. How's that for nuts?

SO WHAT ARE YOU GOING TO DO ABOUT IT?

Why do I tell you this and what does it all mean? It's not to depress you. It's simply to give you a graphic glimpse of the real world.

If you're going to tackle this topsy-turvy job market, deal with the issues straight on. Have no illusions about it. As my journalist buddy T. "Pete" Bonner pointed out recently at a local watering hole, "It's a crazy world that hasn't gotten any saner in 12 centuries." A true poet. I couldn't have put it better myself. If the world isn't fair, what makes you think the job market is any different?

The reality is it's a tough market for everyone, young and old. The message is, older workers have different hurdles to jump. Yet the barriers are not insurmountable. In fact, you'll soon see you have more going for you than you realize. Every older worker is a potential gold mine to an employer. Stick with me and I'll show you how.

STRAIGHTEN UP YOUR ATTITUDE AND DON'T WIMP OUT

More crippling than a tough, biased job market is a self-defeating attitude. It's a basic: If you think you're not going to get a job, *you won't*. So straighten out your head before pounding the pavement. Balancing every age-bias anecdote is a success story in which older workers capture jobs for all the right reasons. It's happening all over America—even in your own backyard.

If you're going to compete with younger workers as well as your peers, understand the issues before tailoring appropriate strategies to counter them. To use a military analogy, don't attack your enemy until you've studied every inch of the battlefield. Hence, the purpose of these introductory chapters.

DEFEAT IS A SELF-FULFILLING PROPHECY

Don't overestimate prospective employers. They won't know how talented and capable you are until you tell them. But they'll surely pick up your negative vibes by looking in your eyes, shaking your hand, and reading your body language. Every day, millions of older job seekers unknowingly telegraph defeat, despair, and hopelessness. Rather than programming themselves for success, they unwittingly set themselves up for failure. A myopic view of their own condition destroys their chances of finding another job. Their defeatist minds bank only stories of colleagues' rejections.

It's your call. If you don't think you stand a chance because the world is out to get you, you've wasted money on this book. A shrink, or better yet a sympathetic bartender, can do more for you than I can. But if you believe talent, intelligence, and creativity will win out, you've made a worthwhile investment.

I truly believe that vivid dreams, fantasies, and visions fueled by hard work can be realized. I've seen it happen countless times. And age was never a barrier. If you want inspiration, pick up a history book and look at the endless list of men and women who changed the world in their fifties, sixties, seventies, and beyond. That ought to propel you into the job market with rocket force.

"I WON'T TAKE IT ANY MORE!"

To make it happen, you'll have to think hard and be tough. In the Oscar-winning film *Network,* an outrageous indictment of the broadcast industry, a network executive (played by Peter Finch) opens a window in his high-rise apartment and screams, "I won't take it any more." In his early sixties, the executive is fired because his superiors feel he is burned out and past his prime. He doesn't agree and is hell-bent on telling the world about it. I'm not suggesting you climb on a soapbox and get militant about your job search. Yet anger and outrage over market injustices ought to fuel you into a job. It will keep the adrenaline coursing through your body, energizing you for the rigors of the job search.

STARTING OVER IS AN OPPORTUNITY

Anything is possible if you truly believe it can be done. As for the prospect of starting over at your age, view it not as a stigma, but as a mouthwatering opportunity. An adventure if you will. I'm not saying this to puff you up. But it's true. You may not realize it, but you have the prized asset all employers want—*experience*. It's so valuable, you often can't even put a price tag on it. Get smart and realize you're a walking, undiscovered treasure. Here's a heartwarming story to prove the point.

A 58-year-old manager who logged over 25 years with major food companies applied for a job as marketing manager of a small specialty food company that was revving up for a new line of health breads. The food company entrepreneur liked the manager's credentials but felt he was overqualified and wouldn't be challenged enough by the job. "Quite frankly, I think someone with 7 to 10 years of marketing experience would best fit this spot," he said. The experienced manager expected this and countered, "Why don't you let me be the judge of that? I know I can help you get this new product line off the ground. I've done it before. Try me out for 6 months and let's see how we work with each other. If it doesn't work out, I'll train my successor before I leave. How does that sound?"

Awed and impressed by the manager's confidence and willingness to submit to a trial period, he agreed. It turned out to be a smart move on the entrepreneur's part. Three months later, the experienced manager had fashioned an ironclad marketing program that captured immediate customer attention. He also took it upon himself to craft an inexpensive advertising/PR program that brought local media coverage.

Needless to say, the entrepreneur thanked his lucky stars he hired the older worker. The happy ending is, less than a year later, the applicant was promoted to vice president with major decision-making power.

Thousands of similar success stories exist. Jim Challenger, president of international outplacement consulting firm Challenger, Gray & Christmas, noted that out-of-work 50-year-old managers are emerging as one of today's preferred groups of employees. "They are the objects of increasing demand by employers seeking experienced talent," he says.

Nevertheless, there is little question that job searching can be tedious and frustrating. Yet it's also exciting, because you don't know where the search will lead. The more effort you put into it, the bigger the rewards. Rather than view it as a downer, see it as a voyage through uncharted waters. Along the way, you'll expand your network and make new friends, while mastering the game and learning more about yourself. Self-discovery is a priceless process.

THE GAME HAS CHANGED

No doubt it's a big crazy world to conquer. Get out there and show them what you can do. It may be a tough, competitive market, but the best part is that the global marketplace has exposed employers to new options. More flexible and less rigid, employers are more willing to take chances, experiment, and listen to profitable strategies. Take the hint and give it to them. After all, who's better qualified to do so?

Above all, lighten up. Don't lose your sense of humor. Taking yourself too seriously is dangerous. Get used to the idea that every day won't be a banner day. There will be days when nothing goes right and you'll wish you could crawl under the covers and hide. Resist that temptation and get real. Don't tell me you never had disastrous days on past jobs. I've had close to a dozen corporate jobs and I can hardly rake up the countless times I fantasized about hurling bosses, clients, or vendors out the window. Face it: People can be infuriating. You're lying to yourself if you're whitewashing the past. No matter what some career writers are peddling, the perfect job is a myth. The trick is coming close to it.

Expect days when you feel blindsided by rejection. Sure it hurts. You wouldn't be human if you weren't momentarily stunned by the disappointment. But don't let it stop you. Get up, lick your wounds, and fight back.

Your ability to bounce back and laugh at the situation will keep you light, buoyant, and sharp. Make no assumptions and have no expectations about your job hunt. You're only setting yourself up for disappointment.

Think of the job hunt as a game. It's not a life-and-death struggle. Play the game tactfully and persistently and you'll win. George Bernard Shaw summed it up nicely when he said, "People who get on in this world deal with circumstances at hand. When those circumstances don't exist, they go out and create them."

Feel better? I've just begun. Wait till I debunk some myths about older workers in the next chapter.

CHAPTER

TWO

"DON'T TELL ME I'M REDUNDANT"

The process of maturing is an art to be learned, an effort to be sustained.
By the age of 50 you have made yourself what you are, and if it is good,
it is better than your youth.   MARYA MANNES
More in Anger

Many older workers believe their own press. Brainwashed, they've fallen into the moat thinking they're not as capable as younger workers. What a mistake! It's time to clear the air and get back on the right track. The fact is you're *more* capable and it's been documented countless times.

DISPELLING THE MYTHS

A $4 million, 5-year study conducted by the Commonwealth Fund, a private New York philanthropic organization, concluded that Americans over 55 are an undervalued, disregarded, and untapped resource. It's just one of at least a dozen studies conducted since the mid-1950s that debunk commonly held myths about older workers. Even the experts who have studied the issue admit these myths are ingrained; they defy logic and hard data. Let's look at a few big ones.

MYTH: Older workers are expensive.

REALITY: Their health-care costs are about the same as those of younger workers. Also, older workers have fewer dependents than younger workers. Studies conclude that human resources professionals do not perceive the cost of older workers to be a problem. In fact, they see such workers as being cost-effective, thus overwhelmingly supporting the notion that the cost of older workers is justified when you consider their value to the company.

MYTH: Older workers are not as productive as younger workers.

REALITY: They're more productive because they make fewer mistakes.

MYTH: Older workers have more on-the-job accidents.

REALITY: They're more careful and have fewer accidents than younger workers.

MYTH: With higher rates of absenteeism and turnover, older workers are generally more unreliable than younger workers.

REALITY: Compared with younger workers, older workers are five times more likely to stay on the job.

MYTH: Older workers are resistant to change and less willing to accept technological advances.

REALITY: A recent IBM study found that workers over 45 adapt more easily to job change than do younger ones. What is often diagnosed as resistance to new ideas among older workers is actually a skepticism borne of experience.

MYTH: Older workers use outmoded work methods.

REALITY: They utilize more advanced skills, learn faster, and are more open to adopting new work methods than younger workers.

MYTH: Older workers have a poor attitude toward their work.

REALITY: With many years of experience behind them, they tend to be more secure about themselves. Harvey Sterns and Michael McDaniel, specialists in industrial gerontology at the University of Akron, report that older workers tend to be more satisfied with their jobs and have a stronger work ethic than younger workers.

What's more, older workers know their priorities and don't feel they have to prove themselves. Unlike younger workers, they've tamed their egos, which is no simple feat.

MYTH: Older workers don't take criticism well.

REALITY: Unlike their younger counterparts, older workers are more open to criticism, leading to self-improvement.

MYTH: Older workers are opinionated and set in their ways, and thus don't work well in group situations.

REALITY: Savvy about group dynamics, older workers are better equipped to sidestep the booby traps of organizational politics. They've mastered the art of playing corporate games.

That's only part of the story. Unlike younger workers, older workers offer multiple skills, an attribute prized by small- to medium-size employers that need workers who can wear more than one hat.

More important, older workers are generally considered to be more creative and better problem solvers. According to researchers, on-the-job creativity takes 10 percent inspiration and 90 percent perspiration. Seasoned older workers are more apt to stick with a problem until it's solved. They've learned the benefits of sweat equity.

Put it all together and it's easy to see why older workers make incredible mentors. They've been playing that role since Adam landed his first corporate job. In the divine order of things, that's the way it ought to be. Just as kids depend on their parents to explain the ways of the world to them, older workers will always be wellsprings of knowledge for younger colleagues. Not even age-bias barriers can prevent that from happening.

YOU'RE NOT GETTING OLDER—YOU'RE GETTING BETTER!

Read that heading again. Now say it aloud. In fact, like the executive in the film *Network,* open your window and scream it to anyone who'll listen. Don't be concerned if anyone hears you or not. Most important is *your* believing it. You're not losing your edge; you're getting better. Make that the affirmation and leitmotif guiding your life. Tattoo it on to your psyche and you'll never doubt your abilities again.

Now you're ready to move to the next chapter and tell Big Blue to take a hike.

HEY BIG BLUE, GO TAKE A HIKE!

Face it. We're all victims of the era in which we grew up. Every generation is stigmatized by the mood of the times. If you grew up during the 1940s and 1950s, as I did, you feel a sense of entitlement regarding work. Following World War II, America emerged as the savior nation. Our dads came home as conquering heroes, the world safe and secure again. It was time to get back to normal and reach for the American dream—a model family of four, dog, picket fence, and secure 9-to-5 job. What could be neater?

We built this ideal life around a perfect job that we'd keep throughout our career. One job with one company. Many of us believed it for decades, until the roof caved in and corporate America had a shattering nervous breakdown in the mid-1980s. The American corporation was overweight and inefficient. It lost its edge. The repercussions are still being felt today.

MOM AND DAD WERE WRONG

The problem is the 50-plus generation is the victim of an outmoded work ethic. Our folks taught us that hard work and loyalty paid off. My immigrant grandfather thought his boss was God because he gave him a job 3 days after my grandfather landed on Ellis Island with a battered suitcase, tattered clothes, and big dreams. My father felt the same way about his employer. Yes, even I was a victim of the same thinking until the day I was deemed redundant and "downsized." At the time, I wasn't quite sure what that term meant. It sounded like a disease. Before I knew what was happening, I was figuring out how long my severance pay would last and the amount of my first unemployment insurance check. Nothing like a chilling shower of corporate reality to give you a new take on life.

So much for the American dream. It was 1986 and the world was changing in front of my eyes. I too thought big American corporations were bastions of strength, indestructible Rocks of Gibraltar, the machinery that kept the entire world revolving on its axis. They were supposed to be the Big Mama nurturing the faithful until the final cadence sounded. I was wrong.

The company epitomizing the myth of job security is IBM, better known as Big Blue. As the first American corporation to develop the policy of lifetime employment, its "no fire" policy became the foundation of corporate paternalism. When the marketplace changed, IBM was already a cumbersome behemoth weighted down in bureaucracy. Competitors that were smarter and faster on their feet gnawed away at Big Blue's flesh. By the mid-1980s, the company had lost its muscle as the ultimate American corporation. It could no longer compete on the corporate battlefield.

To say IBM fell on hard times is an understatement. Pummeled and kicked by a merciless computer industry rocketing toward the twenty-first century, helpless giant Big Blue reeled and stumbled against global cutthroat competition. The corporate titan began hemorrhaging and there were no sutures big enough or strong enough to stop the bleeding.

Former chairman Thomas B. Watson, Jr., son of IBM's founder, expressed shock and surprise that the unwieldy computer maker lost its grip. Like all IBM bigwigs, Watson thought the company was invincible, immortal, impervious to hard times. Come hell or high water, the company would endure. A throwback to a simpler era, Watson was out of touch. IBM's fall from grace is a sad story indeed. Launched in 1956, it was heralded as the perfect company. A job at IBM was considered an honor. You were part of the working elite. Not any more. In 1986, IBM employed 407,000. Now it employs 112,000. Last year alone, the company shed over 40,000 jobs.

THE NEW ORDER

So began a new era and the explosion of a widely held myth. In its heyday, IBM was more than a solid company selling quality products. It offered its workers an enviable lifestyle. For other companies, it was a model, symbolizing egalitarian hiring and business standards.

For 40-odd years following World War II, thousands of

American companies followed IBM's lead, offering workers their own lifetime contract variation. Job security became the centerpiece of the good life. But it proved only to be a "blip in time," as Dan Lacey, late editor and publisher of *Workplace Trends Newsletter,* put it. It was an aberration, an accident never to be repeated. By the late 1980s, the Organization Man was officially drummed out of the American consciousness. Part of a bygone era, he was never to return. The mobile society described by Alvin Toffler (*Future Shock*) became the new reality. The solid citizen who would hold one job on one career path was replaced by the rootless worker who'd have 8 to 10 jobs and undergo two to three career changes throughout his or her life.

American workers have been thrust into a strange new world. With fax machines, cellular phones, notebook computers, and modems, they're learning to job-hunt through cyberspace on the vast information superhighway as telecommuting citizens of the global community. Meanwhile, high-profile companies continue to clean house, permanently laying off tens of thousands of loyal workers.

GET SMART—THINGS WILL NEVER BE THE SAME

I could get real gory and run through a litany of household-name companies that mercilessly fired millions in order to stay profitable. But you get the idea. Actually, I drew a graphic picture of the last four decades to cheer you up. No, I'm not a sadist. I'm an optimist. I sprinted through the past half-century to show you the light—and a radiant light it is.

See yourself in historical perspective. You're part of the story. You're a witness to one of the most significant periods of economic change this country has ever seen. You were there. Your kids and grandchildren will read about you. Americans are no longer doing business and working the way they did two decades ago.

Rather than see it as a curse, see it as a blessing, a new morning, a chance to start over and think differently. Forget the old path and find a new one. You've heard it thousands of times from the self-help hucksters, but it's true. Change is good and healthy. It's like a cold refreshing shower on a sultry summer day. Yes, it's also a shock and it can be difficult. Yet practically everything worthwhile requires some angst and sweat. Face it. If you could reach out and grab everything you wanted, what fun would it be? Believe it or not, we unconsciously enjoy the struggle because it challenges us.

DEPROGRAM YOURSELF

There you have it. It's time to abandon that feeling of entitlement you were raised on. Forget what your folks told you. Stop idealizing the past. More important, stop living in it. The free rides are over. If you want the proverbial gold ring on the merry-go-round of life, you must grab for it yourself.

Deprogram yourself and tell Big Blue and every company like it to take a hike. They lied to you by not making good on their promise. Worse still, in the process of firing you, they copped out by resorting to doublespeak rather than explaining what was happening in plain English. You were dubbed a "negative deficit" and "released," "nonretained," "dehired," or "selected out" in order to "eliminate redundancies in the human resources area" and "enhance efficiency of operations."

Yet you learned some important lessons in the process. Uppermost, companies shouldn't make promises they can't keep and you shouldn't be so gullible and believe everything you're told. All you can expect from a job is the chance to do something you enjoy, fair pay, and (if you're lucky) decent benefits and some near-term security. Anything else is pure gravy. Why should it be any different? A company is not a parent. There is no biological or emotional bond. It's just business, plain and simple. It doesn't take a Keynesian scholar to know that profits are more important than people.

Don't think of me as cold and cynical. That's just the way the world works. It's the divine order. If anything, we've gone back to an honest way of working. Finally, all of us know where we stand and how we fit into the business equation. The message is, rely on yourself. You and only you are responsible for your fate.

Put it all together and you're left with a powerful word: *opportunity*. And a wonderful word it is. It spells new adventures, experiences, a chance to learn new tricks. If that doesn't keep you young, feisty, and excited, I don't know what will. If you doubt me, consider the alternative. Nothing is worse than stagnation.

Now let's rally the troops so we don't have to go it alone.

DON'T ATTEMPT TO DO IT ALONE

No man is an island.   JOHN DONNE (1572–1631)

Now that we've told Big Blue and companies like it where to go, let's get our act together and lay the foundation for our job search.

Start off on the right foot by not making the common mistake of attempting to go it alone. Martyrdom is lonely, not to mention painful. You'll receive no rewards or accolades for it either. Secret sufferers don't win points with the big one upstairs. As I said earlier, you're not alone. Millions of others are in an identical boat.

Sure, it's hard asking for help. Our generation was raised to take care of ourselves. My dad insisted I be tough, macho, streetwise. He told me to fight my own battles, go it alone, rely on my own instincts. So what if I got the stuffing kicked out of me every so often and experienced daily doses of stinging rejection? Hey, those were the breaks and that's the way life worked. So why be a wimp and cry about it? In short, broadcasting weakness of any kind was considered a cardinal sin. Clearly not 1990s thinking.

IT'S OKAY TO BE HUMAN

Thankfully, times and attitudes have changed. The human race has been freed. We can let all our emotions hang out and be ourselves. We can cry, get angry, or lie down on the floor and have screaming temper tantrums.

Thanks to the powerful women's movement, female workers can be assertive and aggressively compete on the business front and in politics. Capitol Hill bureaucrats even gave women pilots permission to fly fighter jets in battle.

Gays no longer have to pretend they're straight. They may not be totally accepted, but at least they're no longer ostracized and barred from jobs. The law is finally on their side. Long overdue.

And men? Thanks to writers like John Bradshaw and Robert Bly, they're also getting into the act. Even though many are still resisting, a vocal minority are finding their feminine sides, making peace with their dads, joining encounter groups, and discovering it's "okay" to express their innermost feelings and fears. A true 1990s man can make a killer meal, wash dishes, change his infant's diapers, and have his manhood challenged at weekly group therapy sessions with his wife. He's even come to terms with the fact that he has to give up Wednesday night poker games with the guys to babysit for his kids. Now that's change.

RELEARN AN OLD SKILL

With all this transition working for us, it shouldn't be difficult to build a solid support front, easing the burdens and frustrations of the job hunt.

Still, chances are it's been a long time since you've pounded the pavement searching for work. All the more reason that you need as much support and encouragement as you can get. Job hunting is difficult for anyone, but it can be especially tedious if you've been out of the job market for a couple of decades. Take it from a pro. It's not that difficult once you get the hang of it.

As you'll soon discover, job searching can't be a part-time effort. It's got to be an obsession and become *your life*. The more allies you have in your corner, the easier it will be.

BUILD A WALL OF SUPPORT ON SEVERAL FRONTS

Keep in mind that different people can serve different functions. The more people you have to share your feelings and job-hunting experiences with, the better. Here are some key sources.

Family

Your home ought to be a safe haven, a combination oasis and comfort zone. This is the place where you can drop the act, stop playing the game, and just hang out and be yourself. Your family is your bulwark, your foundation and source of emotional sustenance.

Don't leave family members out. It's unfair to yourself—and to them. After all, they're part of your grand scheme. Needless to say, they're affected both emotionally and financially by your unemployment. Include them in every step of the process. Share victories and disappointments with them. They deserve to know what's happening.

And when nothing seems to be going right and you feel like throwing in the towel and heading to the Canadian Rockies, they'll be there to boost your ego. So don't be foolish. Your greatest allies are right in your own backyard.

Friends

Don't shut the door on friends. Don't be embarrassed about talking to a trusted friend about your job hunt. Like family, good friends sincerely care and want to help you in any way they can. When you are enmeshed in an exhausting job hunt, there will be times when you'll just want to get away from it all for an evening. A good friend is the ideal person to seek out. You're only human. You simply need to recharge your batteries with a few beers and some laughs before hitting the pavement again.

Support Groups

The past decade has seen a proliferation of self-help support groups, serving every conceivable need and problem, from Survivors of Incest Anonymous and Mothers Against Drunk Drivers to the model for all support groups, Alcoholics Anonymous. There are over half a million support groups in the United States, boasting over 15 million members. And in the next few years, support group membership is expected to escalate dramatically. For good reason. In a complex society burdened with countless stresses, support groups are an accessible, cost-free solution available to anyone. They offer a place where people suffering from the same problem can nurture, learn from, and help one another. In a turbulent corporate environment that continues to pare its ranks of older workers, thousands of displaced professionals have sought solace in support groups. Who better to commiserate with than peers in the same situation?

Support groups for unemployed older workers are popping up in every major city of the United States. And they're easy to find. Many states have self-help clearinghouses that track and monitor groups.

All it takes is a phone call to find a group that can help you out. Also, many churches, synagogues, and nonprofit organizations like the YMCA, YWCA, YMHA, and YWHA offer a variety of support services.

Forty Plus, for example, a nonprofit organization dedicated to helping middle-aged, outplaced executives find new jobs, offers members support groups plus a raft of other services. See the Information Sources at the end of this book for information about Forty Plus, including the addresses and telephone numbers of its 22 chapters across the United States.

CREATE YOUR OWN MUTUAL SUPPORT GROUP

If none of these support styles appeal to you, nothing is preventing you from forming your own mutual support group. Many former corporate managers have enjoyed pouring surplus energy into getting small groups off the ground. It's easier than you think. A group can be started by running a three- or four-line ad in a local weekly or by posting a notice on a community bulletin board. Meeting space is easier to find than you realize. Explain the purpose of the group, and you'll be pleasantly surprised when schools, churches, banks, and even small companies agree to donate a room. Then it's up to you to harness your organizational and problem-solving skills to focus the group members on achieving some mutual goals.

Beyond sharing similar experiences, members can report on different sectors of the job market, passing on hints and tips. One job hunter's experiences can serve as valuable lessons for others. You'd be surprised how valuable these meetings can be. If a meeting serves no other purpose than to exchange battle talk from peers in the same fight, it's well worth your time.

Now that everything is falling into place, let's figure out precisely what types of jobs to find.

WHAT ON EARTH DO YOU WANT?

I know you're anxious to beat the bushes searching for a job. But be patient, because there are a few more preliminary steps to get you on the right track.

As I said, you've got a lot going for you. Be glad you're not the average job searcher peddling 5 to 10 years of experience. Many of you, thankfully, have severance packages and pensions that will keep the wolf at bay for a while. That puts you at a wonderful vantage point. You've got the luxury to hang back and sample the market until the best deal surfaces.

Even if your financial situation is not as secure, I urge you to think very carefully about what you want.

OPPORTUNITY OF A LIFETIME: WHAT ARE YOUR GOALS?

Remember what I said in Chap. Three. You've got an open sea in front of you. You can swim slowly and steadily and search for a similar job, or you can ride the waves and play it dangerously by taking chances you've always dreamed about.

You can do anything you want. Chances are your kids are grown up and out of the house. Now that's something to celebrate. What better time to try for something that will truly make you happy? So don't even attempt to come to a quick decision. Instead, carefully consider your options.

"I NEVER KNEW I HAD SO MANY CHOICES"

Start by putting your options down on paper so you can absorb them. Things take on a whole new reality when you see them in writing. The best part is once you start writing, thoughts and ideas will pop into your head that you never considered before.

Following are some paths that 50-plus job searchers have taken.

1. *Pick up where you left off.*   If you loved your prior job, there is no harm in searching for the same kind of position. If you worked for a large company, for example, consider looking at a similar position in smaller companies that might better appreciate your talents.

Later on we'll take a closer look at the advantages of working for small versus big companies. It's up to you to weigh the pros and cons of each.

2. *Change organizations.*   If you've worked for profit-making companies all your life, consider pursuing nonprofit or government organizations. Each has its own culture and rules, worlds apart from the typical corporation. More about the sprawling nonprofit world later on.

3. *Relocate.*   After living in one place most of your life, you may be struck with wanderlust and hanker to test a new location. Welcome to the mobile society, in which millions of workers relocate for new opportunities every year. Some cities offer better job opportunities for 50-plus workers. A handful of midwestern cities, for instance, boast practically no unemployment. Better yet, the demand for workers exceeds the supply. Sounds like utopia. That means job searchers practically call the shots. The unemployment rate in Sioux Falls, SD, is 1.9 percent—the lowest in the nation. But other cities boast equally impressive unemployment rates. The accompanying tables list metropolitan areas with the lowest and highest unemployment rates. Take a good look. If nothing else, it's food for thought.

4. *Play the field.*   Maybe you're restless and bored and need to test the water before settling into a serious job. After all, you've spent most of your career at one or two jobs. After being loyal to a fault, you may want to sample different work settings. It's only natural. By all means, do so by checking out the part-time and temporary markets.

U.S. Cities With the Lowest Unemployment

Sioux Falls, SD	1.9%
Madison, WI	2.0
Fargo-Moorhead, ND	2.0
Iowa City, IA	2.3
Minneapolis–St. Paul, MN	2.5
Sioux City, IA	2.5
Des Moines, IA	2.5
Rochester, MN	2.6
Nashville, TN	2.8
Raleigh–Durham–Chapel Hill, NC	2.8
Omaha, NE	2.8
Grand Forks, ND	2.9
St. Cloud, MN	2.9
Fayetteville–Springdale–Rogers, AR	2.9

U.S. Cities With the Highest Unemployment

Modesto, CA	14.5%
McAllen–Edinburg–Mission, TX	14.2
Fresno, CA	12.0
Bakersfield, CA	11.8
Brownsville–Harlingen–San Benito, TX	11.2
Stockton-Lodi, CA	11.0
Vineland–Millville–Bridgeton, NJ	11.0
Jersey City, NJ	9.9
Beaumont–Port Arthur, TX	9.8
El Paso, TX	9.8
Atlantic City–Cape May, NJ	9.7
Los Angeles–Long Beach, CA	9.7
Danville, VA	9.4
Taxarkana, TX	9.2

SOURCE: U.S. Bureau of Labor Statistics.

THE NEW CONTINGENT WORK FORCE

A volatile job market has created a new employment category called the *contingent worker*, a fancy term for part-time, just-in-time, temporary, and self-employed staff. According to the U.S. Bureau of Labor Statistics, the contingent work force has grown 57 percent since 1980. That's three times faster than the labor force as a whole. The contingent worker is sort of an educated, better-paid version of the classic migrant worker.

In Silicon Valley, California's high-tech nerve center, many displaced executives are doing well taking short-term assignments ranging from 6 months to a couple of years. Actually, they're renting themselves out to companies on the way up or on the way out or to start-up and established companies with critical short-term needs. The modern business world's equivalent of hired guns, they're taking their hard-earned talents and selling them to the highest bidder. Most of these corporate refugees are in their early to mid-fifties.

It's no surprise that State of the Art Computing Inc., a San Diego firm created to manage such rented technical managers, is doing a brisk business. If a company has a new product and needs a dynamite product development team to get it off the ground, State of the Art Computing will round up the cream of the crop. The downside is you'll have to contend with a lot of stress, and there are no benefits. But if it's well-paid, brief bursts of excitement you crave, this arrangement could make you very happy. Companies like State of the Art Computing are popping up all over the country. Nose around and you'll find them.

That's only for starters. When we explore the new world of temping, later on, you'll discover work options that never existed a decade ago.

If none of the above appeals to you, maybe you're revving up for a career change—a major issue deserving a chapter by itself. Career changing became a big trend in the 1980s. Yet in the 1990s sociologists predict career changers' ranks will skyrocket. Once again, we can thank the turbulent corporate battlefield for making it happen, plus the quest for improving the quality of our lives. The search for the meaning of life continues. No wonder an idealistic minority is turning its back on the almighty buck in search of true career satisfaction. One surefire way to achieve this goal is through a career change.

Let's find out how to do it.

"I WANT TO BE AN ASTRONAUT"

I don't know any 50-year-old astronauts. But who said you can't be the first? Just because it's never been done doesn't mean it's impossible. Right?

ARE YOU SURE YOU'RE UP FOR A CAREER CHANGE?

Not exactly. Be realistic. Radical career changes are made every day. Doctors and attorneys are becoming carpenters and innkeepers, while computer programmers and social workers are becoming stockbrokers. I even met a nun who became—are you ready?—an FBI agent.

But if a vocation requires strenuous physical effort, such as that demanded of astronauts, you may have to forget about it. Sorry. That doesn't mean the curtain comes down on your life. That's just plain old reality reminding us we're human and can't do all the things we were capable of doing when we were younger.

I'm a classic example. Every so often I enjoy some incredible Walter Mitty fantasies about being a world-class biker and racing in the famed Tour de France. I envision crossing the finish line with both hands stretched out above my head, acknowledging the cheering crowds while Aaron Copeland's *Fanfare for the Common Man* blares from stadium-size speakers.

Don't laugh. I'm a damned good biker, particularly if you tack on the inevitable qualifier—"for my age." If superstar racer Greg LeMonde quit in the middle of the 1994 Tour de France at the age of 33—which is considered old for a bike racer—what do you think my chances are at 50? The answer is, dismal. Even if I actually completed the grueling Tour de France, by the time I crossed the finish line, spectators would have forgotten about the race. There'd be no one to applaud me but my family and my parrot.

You get the point. Yes, anything is possible in this best of all worlds—if you meet the criteria. If it's doable, by all means "Just Do It," as the famous Nike ad says. If you don't, you'll beat yourself up for not trying.

DO YOU MEAN CAREER CHANGING OR SALVAGING?

These days, job changing has practically been elevated to a sport. *Career changing* is something else. It has always gotten a lot of press. Richard Bolles and other career writers make it seem so easy. Just ask yourself a bunch of questions to discover what turns you on—or find a career counselor who'll give you a battery of expensive tests—and you're on your way to a career change. Wrong! There is much more to it. Career changing is difficult and complicated. But it's possible if you're ready to commit yourself to the task.

First, let's clear up some confusion and get the terminology right. Career changing is often confused with a certain kind of job switching that I call *career salvaging*. More and more disgruntled job changers are invigorating their careers by switching industries. Bored or disenchanted with one industry, they try their hand at another. *Examples:* Computer programmer moves from aeronautics to film industry. Middle manager laid off in the frenetic software industry shifts to middle management in the aerospace industry.

Granted, these are big changes that involve learning about a new industry. Yet all they require is using identical job skills in a new industry setting.

A career change, on the other hand, is a radical departure in the way you earn your living. *Examples:* Journalist becomes lawyer or programmer. Lawyer becomes cook. Car thief becomes check forger.

In any career change, you're moving to a field which requires new skills. Hopefully, you have the aptitude and personality for your new career. Nevertheless, it means starting over in an entry-level position. You're going back to school and learning a field from the ground up. You're starting at the beginning of the alphabet. No matter how you romanticize it, that ain't easy.

This brings us to the reality of career-changing statistics.

Putting the hype about career changing aside, I'd take the statistics with a grain of salt. The U.S. Bureau of Labor Statistics reports that 10 percent of the work force changes careers every year. James Challenger, president of the Chicago outplacement firm of Challenger, Gray & Christmas, says it's half that amount. I'll take a conservative stance at somewhere between the two.

Remember, a thriving niche industry has started helping people change careers. Blame it for some of the inflated statistics. When all is said and done, career changing is possible if you know what you're doing. One thing is certain: Each year more 50-year-olds are contemplating a career change. Whether they actually go through with it is another matter.

TO SWITCH OR NOT TO SWITCH

Ever wonder why some people do mental cartwheels over the prospect of changing careers while others reject the idea entirely? It hinges on having an all-consuming desire to radically change your life by earning a living doing something different. Some of the reasons both for and against career switching make perfectly good sense. Let's take a look at this new battlefield and find out whether you're up for the joust.

Why People Change Careers

Let's start with the reasons that people switch careers.

1. *Technological change.* Say you had a secure job in an old-line manufacturing firm that became automated over a 6-month period, thus eliminating better than 50 percent of the jobs. If it was just a matter of time before your place in the production process was usurped by a computer, you'd have no choice but to bail out and find a new career. Simply put, changing jobs is only a temporary maneuver. Inevitably, you'll have to retool yourself for a new career.

All industries have been affected by technology. For instance, it once took a half-dozen bookkeepers and administrative assistants to keep an office's records up to date. Today a totally automated office with one computer and three clerks can turn out at least twice as much work.

2. *Failing company.*   Faltering companies force many disillusioned workers into new careers. There's no point running through the litany of companies that went the way of all flesh in the past decade. I guarantee it would fill the rest of this book—and then some. When the paychecks are coming regularly, it's easy to delude yourself into thinking you enjoy what you're doing. But when the company is going under and you risk losing your job, suddenly the sky opens up, the sea parts, and you ask yourself, "Why in the world would I look for the same type of job when it bores me to death?"

Once past the confusion and uncertainty, not to mention immobilizing fear, you ponder the prospects of doing something you actually enjoy.

3. *Failing industry.*   The same rationale applies to a crumbling industry. Imagine you've been part of the widget industry since the late 1950s. Now it's falling apart before your eyes. You're a victim of what the experts call *structural unemployment*—the condition of permanent unemployment created by the phasing out of old jobs and the creation of new ones as a result of technological change.

You're forced into making a move. You've got two choices. If you love what you're doing, you can shift your skill to another industry. This is an example of career salvaging, mentioned earlier. But if you're ready to move on, an overall career change makes sense.

4. *Unhappiness.*   Under the umbrella heading of unhappiness, I'll include disillusionment, disinterest, boredom, and changing values and motivation. It's amazing when you consider the staggering number of workers who despise their jobs. One morning, they drag themselves out of bed and say to themselves, "I can't take it any longer. I'm quitting." What brought them to that point is the stuff that makes shrinks wealthy. It just proves that people are complicated and unpredictable. What drove us in our twenties is no longer important in our forties and fifties. Reason enough to downshift into something that revs up our juices.

5. *Money.*   Even in the get-in-touch-with-yourself 1990s, nothing is wrong with switching careers for money. After all, when you cut through the pretense, one of the pressing reasons for changing jobs is financial. The fact is that some careers pay better than others. Take the writing business. What kind of fool goes into it for the bucks? Yes, there are superstars making incredible money. But they're the exception. Most full-time independent writers are struggling to make ends meet. Others do something else full time and write in their spare time. Or, if lucky, they are supported by spouses or trust funds.

That's just one dramatic example. I've known many disillusioned teachers who threw in the towel because wages were abysmally low. Some became stockbrokers or lawyers so they could enjoy a better lifestyle.

You get the picture. Throw all the idealistic patter that's been rammed down your throat out the window and look at the money issue honestly. It's no crime switching careers for more money—if you *enjoy* what you're going to be doing. If you don't, you'll have problems later on.

6. *Power and prestige.*   Right alongside the desire for money, the need for power and prestige is a compelling force by itself. As you master your new career, you stand a good chance of ascending to a powerful position. It's very common when switching from a profit-making to a nonprofit company. A low-level manager who becomes a superstar fund raiser in a nonprofit organization garners enormous power and respect, because he or she becomes critical to the organization's survival. For the same reason, the position carries well-deserved prestige.

7. *Personal reasons.*   Life deals us unexpected twists and turns. A divorced parent who gains custody of his or her children and is not earning enough to support the family may change careers to meet newfound needs. In short, circumstances often dictate our career direction. The tough part is picking the right career road.

8. *Health or age.*   Certain industries are more hazardous than others. The construction and oil and gas industries are two that come to mind. If you're working at a physically demanding job in these industries—as an engineer or a field manager, for example—poor health could impede your performance and trigger a career change. The same goes for age. Blame it on genetic makeup, but some of us are stronger than others. Many 50- and 60-year-olds change careers when they discover they can no longer work at physically taxing jobs. It's just nature telling them they've got to find a new career.

Why People Don't Switch Careers

For many people, a career change represents a new chapter in life. Yet many others avoid it, for the following reasons.

1. *Fear of the unknown.*   Fear is the greatest single force preventing people from doing anything. A fear of making fools of ourselves or not succeeding keeps millions of us locked into tedious, dead-end careers. I'm not going to play shrink and attempt to explain how fear can stop us in our tracks. Suffice it to say, it's an immobilizing force with complex origins.

2. *Uncertainties of the job market.*   In a topsy-turvy job market, many potential career changers back off and wait for market conditions to stabilize before considering a major move. Even job changers contemplating the step up to a better job slot proceed cautiously during uncertain periods. If the unemployment rate is going through the roof and industry conditions are shaky, you might not want to risk giving up what you have to venture off in a new direction. Yes, it's healthy to take risks. But often, hanging back makes sense too. It's a judgment call.

3. *Relocation.*   Even though relocation (see Chap. Five) can be a tantalizing and challenging adventure, many older workers avoid it. Families, friends, business relationships, and real estate holdings are all good reasons for not moving. Sentimental and financial attachments are also powerful reasons for staying where you are.

4. *Money.*   Money is a good reason for changing careers, but it's also a good reason to remain at the job. If you're conflicted about changing careers, as many of us are, money can be the deciding factor—especially if you're earning a good salary. Some of us value money more than others. You may not love your work all that much, but the money is satisfying. A stockbroker friend confessed he occasionally has ideological battles with himself. There are times when he hates selling and the frustrations of dealing with temperamental and difficult clients. Yet the feeling is always overridden by his sizable commissions, which give him a lifestyle that would be hard to duplicate doing something more fulfilling. He knows a career change means starting over—with drastically lower earnings. That translates to dramatically downgrading his lifestyle—a compromise he's not willing to make.

The moral of the story is don't be too harsh on yourself if you feel the same way.

REVVING YOURSELF UP FOR A CAREER CHANGE

If you've decided to change careers, go into it with your eyes open. As I said, career changing isn't easy. Be prepared for rough seas. There'll be days when everything is rocking smoothly along, but there'll also be days when you feel like the waves are crashing down on your head. At times like these, you'll rue the day you decided to change careers: "What made me do it? I must have been out of my mind."

Here's what you can expect.

1. *Criticism, resistance, and opposition.* As much as you want support and backing from everyone around you, don't expect it. As excited as you are about bounding ahead with your new career, some people will think you're nuts. Just when you ask for friendly advice from an old schoolmate, she tells you to abandon the project: "You're never going to make it—you know nothing about the business. When you go through the little money you socked away, what then? It's a crapshoot all the way. If you want smart advice, stick with your current career. You'll save yourself an awful lot of aggravation in the end."

Even your spouse may not support your career change: "How could you give up everything you've worked so hard for? You're at the top of your field. You command a top salary, not to mention incredible seniority and respect. By turning your back on it, you're throwing in the towel."

Instead of blatant criticism, be prepared for naysayers tossing old-fashioned guilt in your face: "Hey, Ethel, it sounds great in theory. I'm sure there are thousands of people like yourself who thought they could accomplish the same thing and fell flat on their faces. What if you fail? Have you thought about what you're putting your family through? You're going to take them down with you. What you're doing is pretty selfish."

Like they say, when friends like this are dishing out doomsday advice, who needs enemies? Toughen up and get ready to absorb negative reactions. There is no predicting how people are going to react when you tell them you're contemplating a change and seek their advice. Some may think you've gone off the deep end, while others may be jealous because you've got the guts to do something they only fantasize about doing.

2. *Rejection.* Rejection is part of the job-hunting game. The average job seeker has a tough enough time finding a job; it's twice as hard for the career changer. No matter how determined and talented you are, face facts: Many employers have serious doubts about hiring anyone over 50. Just imagine what they'll think of the 50-year-old career changer who spent 10 or 20 years doing something else.

You may be rejected several times before you land an acceptable job. You may experience intense frustration because employers never give you straight answers. Like I said, get tough. Rejection is part of the game and there is nothing you can do but absorb it, learn from it, and most important not let it squelch your enthusiasm.

3. *Periods of self-doubt, despair, despondency, and depression.* Self-doubt is often the aftermath of rejection. No matter how confident you are, at times you'll doubt yourself and wonder whether you're making the right move. As much as you'd like to remain optimistic and charged, some days nothing will seem to go right. You'll get rejection letters from employers and, worse yet, second-party turndowns from their assistants. You'll spend days working up lengthy proposals for unique business concepts only to have them rejected after a superficial reading. You'll become depressed because no one will give you the time of day. Clearly, it takes a strong ego to overcome setbacks like these. There'll be despondent days when you feel like wailing the blues from sunrise to sunset.

Sounds pretty grim. Yet, just when you think the world is coming apart before your eyes, the sun comes out bright and strong, and the world looks more radiant and conquerable. The message is simple: *Stay at the helm and never abandon ship, no matter what kind of treacherous squalls you encounter.*

4. *Lengthy periods of inaction.* Get used to the idea that things seldom happen quickly, especially in large companies. Decisions are rarely made by one person. Small companies take action faster because there are fewer decision makers. But even there, you're relegated to a bottom-of-the-pile decision. And then there is the interview process, which can amount to several interviews spaced over 2 or 3 weeks. All things considered, it could be months before a decision is made. Like it or not, waiting is part of the game. Smart career changers learn early in the game that it's important to keep busy every minute of the day.

5. *Setbacks.*   Expect a few setbacks as well. Just when you thought you were making inroads, something unexpected happens and you're back to square one. No matter how meticulously you plan your career change, there will be days, even weeks, when nothing seems to go right. See these setbacks as temporary barricades and get back to the business at hand.

THINK TWICE ABOUT HIRING A CAREER COUNSELING FIRM

Now that you know what to expect, here are some thoughts on career counselors.

Most career changers go about the process by themselves. They stumble and fall, but eventually wind up crossing the finishing line on their own. A small minority opt for help.

Plenty of companies out there would love to help you change careers—for a fee, of course. Two cautionary words: *Be careful.* Check your local paper and you'll see ads for a variety of career services. The people who run these firms call themselves anything from career counselors, career managers, transition experts, career guidance professionals, and career guidance executives to recruitment advisers, recruitment consultants, and professional career consultants.

Your mission is separating the wheat from the chaff. A reliable career counselor helps identify skills and aptitudes and develops job-hunting techniques. You're paying for professional assistance, nothing more. *Career counselors can't get you jobs.* However, many less-than-scrupulous career counseling outfits lead clients to believe they can get them jobs. Not only are these outfits incapable of finding jobs, but clients are hardly sent out on interviews. Better business bureaus and state attorney general's offices have received thousands of complaints about fraudulent counseling firms. In some cases, they've uncovered high-pressure sales tactics, ridiculously priced aptitude-testing and letter-writing services, and implied promises of employment that were never met.

The problem is, career counseling firms are virtually unregulated. That's why picking a legitimate counseling firm requires thought and effort. To make the best decision, consider the following tips.

1. *Make a list of 5 to 10 career professionals who might be able to help you.*   Initially, call the career professionals to find out about their services and whether they provide a free consultation. If they charge for a consultation or are overly insistent upon seeing you before volunteering any information over the phone, thank them for their time and cross them off your list. A professional outfit should be more than happy to provide as much information as possible over the phone. And the majority of reputable career counselors will give you a free consultation. If the vibes are good, schedule an appointment.

2. *Ask what they charge.*   Fees range from a very modest $50 way up into the thousands. Don't make the mistake of equating expensive with quality. You can pay over $3000 for a comprehensive workshop and individual coaching that can last 2 months and have your life rejuvenated in the process. Or you can find yourself in the same place you started, only $3000 poorer. The question is: What exactly do you get for your money?

3. *Beware of guarantees.*   If the counselor makes exaggerated guarantees, promising instant results, head for the door. You're dealing with a huckster.

4. *Check out the program.*   In your face-to-face meeting, ask the career counselor to spell out exactly what the program is all about. Find out whether it meets your needs. Check out the counselor's background and ask yourself: "Can this person actually help me? Does the program make sense or am I being conned with flowery hype?"

5. *Beware of high-pressure tactics.*   If the person tries to give you the rush act or is intent on having you sign on the dotted line before leaving, grab your attaché case and leave. Many less-than-reputable career counselors are expert at creating a sense of urgency, subtly intimidating you into signing up for their crash course.

Once you've visited a number of career counselors, sort out your information, replay conversations, and then go with your instincts. They won't deceive you.

Let's push on and find out about the benefits of thinking like an entrepreneur.

THINK LIKE AN ENTREPRENEUR

Entrepreneurs are a fascinating bunch. The more interesting ones are bona fide nuts. That's one of the reasons I enjoy writing about them. Over the past decade I've written countless pieces about America's top entrepreneurs. Some of the wackiest I've known are obsessive-compulsive overachievers who eat, smoke, drink, and work to excess. Most have the persistence of pit bulls. The only way to stop them from reaching their goals is to shoot them. And I'm not exaggerating.

If you're wondering why I'm rambling about off-the-wall entrepreneurs I've known, stay with me. There is a powerful similarity between launching a business and getting a job. You'd be giving your job search a jet assist by emulating the positive traits of high-performance entrepreneurs. In fact, it wouldn't hurt if you pretend you are one for the next few months. What do you have to lose? Every entrepreneur I've met or read about is a bundle of lessons. Read the biographies of entrepreneurs like Andrew Carnegie, Cornelius Vanderbilt, John D. Rockefeller, and Helena Rubenstein. You'll be inspired. More important, you'll learn from them.

EIGHT TRAITS OF SUCCESSFUL ENTREPRENEURS

Like every entrepreneur, you're working toward a goal. Achieving it means overcoming resistance and hurdling barriers in your way. Get my drift? You may not even realize you have entrepreneurial traits. What better time to get in touch with them than right now? Remember, these are traits that can help you snare jobs.

Here are eight of the most important.

1. *Creativity.*   As the Eastern mystics say, creative energy is a pow-erful life force. All of us are creative, some more so than others. Yet artists, writers, and composers don't have a lock and key on creativi-ty. Creativity also spawned the machines and devices that run our world, not to mention mundane products we take for granted. Successful entrepreneurs ooze creativity from their pores. It's not like the world is waiting to accept the products and services they're selling. They must convince people to buy.

Sound familiar? Aren't you in the same boat? Don't delude your-self—you're a product. Like the entrepreneur packaging a product for market acceptance, you must package yourself. But you must do it better than your competition, of which you have plenty. You're competing against people your own age as well as aggressive younger applicants. Overtaking them will require original, analyti-cal, and independent thinking, which is part of the creative process. Set up any analogy that pleases you. Put yourself on a playing field, on a battlefield, or in front of a chessboard. Winning takes creativity and original thinking that gets results.

2. *Vision.*   Entrepreneurs have a knack for seeing the big picture. They have a vision that gets them up at 5 every morning, keeping their adrenaline pumping at rocket speed all day. You ought to have a similar vision you're passionate about. No matter how tough things get, never give up on turning your vision into reality.

3. *Productivity.*   I don't know of any entrepreneur who had it easy. You've heard the cliché thousands of times: "Nobody ever gave me anything. I had to slave for it myself." Entrepreneurs who've made it big love regurgitating lines like these. Can you blame them? They're proud of their accomplishments.

You should be proud of your experience as well. You don't have to launch a Microsoft or a Snapple to take well-deserved pride in your work. Your major accomplishment could be conquering an impossible sale or finding a solution to what seemed like an unsolv-able computer problem. It could be anything that gave you heartfelt pleasure. Anything worth having takes work and sweat. Why should conquering a great job be different? As my father used to say to me when I cut school or refused to do my homework, "There are no free rides." Maybe the Puritans were right. There's real virtue in hard work.

4. *Resourcefulness.* Right alongside hard work is knowing how to get things done efficiently and quickly. Most entrepreneurs start out underfunded. Creative entrepreneurs, however, are so committed to reaching their goals that they practically beg, borrow, and steal to get the job done. That almost always means cutting corners and finding inventive ways to stretch limited resources. You may be in an identical boat. You may not have a hefty severance package to finance your job hunt, or you may estimate that your funds will run out in 6 weeks. Panicking won't help. Instead, tap available resources to find a way out of the dilemma. Maybe it means serious budgeting, selling the second car (you don't need that gas guzzler, anyway), getting a part-time or temporary job, or making your live-at-home 28-year-old daughter kick money into the pot to make your life easier.

5. *Adaptability and flexibility.* Entrepreneurs abhor rules and routines. They enjoy mapping their own route and not knowing what's around the bend. They have an insatiable appetite for excitement. They love sailing off in a new direction when the entrepreneurial winds suddenly shift. Ross Perot said it's the individual's ability to deal with the unexpected that characterizes the difference between success and failure.

Don't get upset. I know you're not an entrepreneur and you enjoy the security of routines and order. That's fine for later. For now, get used to the idea that there is no divine order to your life. Every day will be different. As hard as you try to get things done in an orderly fashion, there'll be days when chaos reigns. Just as career changers must expect hellish days when nothing goes right, you must too. More important is finding ways to deal with them.

6. *Unconventionality.* Entrepreneurs thrive on breaking the rules. Many are corporate refugees, organizational misfits who couldn't hold a job if their life depended upon it. They're like wild stallions who refuse to be herded. Give them an order and they'll do the opposite for spite. I'm not suggesting you antagonize interviewers or use abrasive tactics that turn people off. Yet no one says you can't use unconventional methods to get your foot in the door. One highly recommended nontraditional tactic is junking your résumé and using a well-written letter instead. More on that later.

7. *Persistence.* Remember my pit bull analogy? It's true. The most committed entrepreneurs never give up. Put them in a labyrinth filled with moats, hidden mines, starving alligators, and charging rhinos and they'll find a way out and enjoy every minute. It's a basic: If you want something badly enough, you find a way to make it happen. Survival almost always takes unrelenting commitment, persistence, and refusal to accept failure.

Several entrepreneurs have spun elaborate theories about the relationship between persistence and the experience of failure. Richard Worth, the freewheeling entrepreneur who runs the Chicago-based cookie company The Delicious Frookie Company, Inc., asserts, "Failure equals success." According to Worth, smart entrepreneurs learn more from their failures than from their successes. But it's persistence that keeps them slugging away no matter what obstacles block their path. Like committed entrepreneurs, you must master this trait. If you doubt me, think about the alternative. Slow down and someone will overtake you. Don't let it happen.

8. *Courage.*   I'm not talking about the kind of courage it takes to go 10 rounds with a mean-looking middleweight or the courage needed to march off to war. It takes a different kind of courage to create something and have enough confidence in it to try to convince others of its uniqueness and value. Entrepreneurs are forced to do this every day. Job searchers face equally forbidding barriers. First is the hassle accompanying the job hunt itself; second is the unavoidable age bias. It takes courage to overcome these hurdles. Courage means believing in yourself enough to muster the emotional strength to cross all barriers. You'll also need stamina, self-assurance, and a cast-iron will.

BE SMART ENOUGH TO GET GOOD ADVICE

Smart entrepreneurs know their limitations. Early on, they discover they can't do it all. They need help and advice to make smart decisions. So they go out and find the best they can. I urge you to think along the same lines. There'll be times when you're stymied and need information. The go-it-aloners often lose precious time stumbling along and making poor decisions. We're living in a sophisticated, complex world where we depend upon others. Don't be pigheaded, stubborn, or lazy. If you need help, ask for it. That's what family, friends, and your network (see Chap. Nine) are for.

Now let's get busy and make time count.

DON'T GET HOOKED ON DAYTIME TALK SHOWS

I'm not embarrassed to admit I'm a TV junkie. A boob-tube addict. A major-league couch potato. I could easily while away an entire day staring at the TV, starting with daytime talk shows and going all the way into the wee hours of the morning with Grade B 1950s movies. If monetary awards were given away for procrastination, I'd be a multimillionaire. What better way to kill time than by curling up in front of the tube with enough junk food and beer to sustain you for a month?

I don't have a patent on "procrastinitis." It's a universal affliction, especially if you don't have to report to a job. So don't be uptight if you're one of the chosen. You have plenty of company.

But hanging out at home won't get you a job. Getting yourself up and out in the morning isn't easy. Nevertheless, I urge you to fight the universal temptation to goof off. Job hunting can't be a part-time effort when the spirit moves you. It must be a full-time, disciplined, compulsive pursuit. So change your thinking immediately. The best way to go about it is by making the job search a job in itself. If it makes you feel better, think of it as a nonpaying job. Do whatever works.

In reality, you could be out of work for several months. How long? The rule of thumb is 4 full-time weeks of job searching for every $10K in compensation. The higher the salary, the narrower the pyramid. At the $100K level, it could take up to a year.

Look at it not as time on your hands, but as an opportunity to immerse yourself in finding a job that turns you on. Get ready, I'm going to make you into a high-powered machine.

GET YOUR ACT TOGETHER

First, you need a place to run your job search. Think of it as your command center, the place where you'll make serious career decisions and do high-powered thinking.

If you don't have a quiet place to work, create one. *Avoid makeshift offices.* Too many job searchers create portable offices wherever they happen to be at the time. One minute they're in a den, the next in the bedroom or basement or on a patio. When in the field, they're running their job search out of their attaché cases. It's mobile for sure, but after a week, you're struggling with chaos. Open that Pandora's Box of an attaché case and out will tumble letters, your appointment book, scraps of paper, files in disarray, a half-eaten doughnut, and who knows what else.

A comfortable place to work in your home can put a whole new spin on your job search. You'll quickly find a reassuring comfort in order. Like any well-run office, yours ought to have all the essentials, including telephone, answering machine, stationery, computer or typewriter (or both), file cabinet, pencils, pens, postage, paper clips, and stapler. The idea is to get up in the morning and get right to work so you don't miss a beat.

The two most essential tools are an answering machine and a day organizer. When you're out in the field, you don't want to lose important calls from potential employers, headhunters, leads, or colleagues. It could be the call you've been waiting for. That answering machine is critical.

Day organizers are great for organizing your business life. Pocket-size or book-style, they help keep your appointments in order when you've got a busy day planned. Everything is right there in front of you—appointments, calendar, addresses, telephone numbers, notes, and important reminders.

KEEP A JOB SEARCH LOG

Order is the name of the game. Once you get into your job search, you'll be pleasantly surprised at how busy you are. You'll be going full tilt making appointments, phone calls, follow-ups—you name it. The best way to track it all and maintain total control is by keeping a job search log. How you do it is up to you. Use a notepad, a typewriter, or better yet a personal computer. To be on top of your job search, make entries daily.

Here are the critical components of a job search log:

- Correspondence (sent or received, with dates)
- Calls (made or received)
- Company
- Contact
- Follow-up
- Status

The last three of these items—contact, follow-up, and status—are especially important. When you're busy and have a lot on your mind, it's easy to forget names and important facts and observations. If you have to return 30 calls over a 5-day period, it's virtually impossible to remember critical facts about each contact.

CREATE A SCHEDULE

Once your office is set up, create a schedule and try to stick with it. As I said in the preceding chapter, be flexible. There'll be times when you are in the field all day or at the library preparing for a killer interview or undergoing an intense round of interviews. The rest of the time, you'll be like a disciplined machine faithful to your schedule.

Advice: Start early so you get the benefit of a long, productive day. Consider this model schedule.

8 a.m. to 12 noon.   Get a cup of coffee and scan the morning papers. The more you read, the better. A couple of dailies and *The Wall Street Journal* should tell you what's happening on the business front. Look at the want ads and business pages, and scan the general news as well. You never know when you'll pick up a lead or a brilliant job-hunting strategy.

Be sure to check the want ads *every day.* Most job searchers read want-ad pages on Wednesday and Sunday, traditionally the busiest days for classified advertising. Yet many perverse employers run ads on other days as well, just to see if they'll stumble on some creative mavericks.

This is the time to think about when you're going to call people and schedule appointments. Knowing when to phone busy company owners and managers is an art in and of itself. People are funny about receiving calls. Some managers never answer their own phones. Others do so at off hours, such as before 9 a.m. or after 5 p.m. when things quiet down. Some have elevated ducking callers to a sport. You're on your own. Be creative. In this high-tech age, it's easy to avoid telephone calls. A secretary is the traditional guardian of the gate, screening all calls. More frustrating is voice mail which hurtles you into a dark chasm of options, never knowing whether anyone will ever receive it or, worse yet, whether your call will ever be returned. At least with a secretary, you stand a chance of leaving an impression and, if you're lucky, finding an ally, so you can pave the way to an actual conversation with the boss.

When you're not scheduling appointments, talk to colleagues and contacts, write letters, and keep your log up to date.

12 noon to 3:30 p.m.   Make good use of the lunch hour. The working world can afford to waste away an hour munching burgers, sandwiches, and soft drinks. You can't. Eat on the run. Fifteen minutes should do it. Lunch is a great time to get from one place to another or do research. Forget about reaching anyone in the corporate world during this period. They're either actually out having lunch or using the time to work undisturbed at their desks. Calls from compulsive job seekers won't be greeted kindly.

To get a more objective and relaxed reception, schedule appointments in the afternoon, preferably between 2 p.m. and 4 p.m. You're taking your chances with morning appointments. Often, they're fraught with confusion and tension. The day is just beginning. Busy entrepreneurs and managers don't know what's ahead and they've yet to find their stride.

Warning: The worst interview day is Monday. Unless business owners need someone desperately, few have the patience to give their undivided attention to a job interview first thing in the week. However, there'll be times when you have no control over the matter and you're forced to see people at their convenience.

4:00 p.m. to 5:30 p.m.   Late afternoon is wrap-up time. When possible, try to get home before the end of the business day to return calls. If you can't, check your answering machine messages from the field so important calls can be returned. Resume chores started in the morning. Send out letters, make entries in your log, or finish any other necessary paperwork.

5:30 p.m. to 6:30 p.m. Before calling it quits, change the pace by getting some exercise. Walk, jog, or bike; play racquetball, tennis, or basketball. They all accomplish the same end. The idea is to do something you enjoy. It's critical for your mental and physical well-being. Exercise is a healthy escape valve, relieving pent-up tension and anxiety. Just getting out of the house relieves the pressure a little. Try to set aside an hour every day for exercise. If that's impossible, try every other day. I guarantee results.

DON'T BE A MARTYR: GIVE YOURSELF A TREAT

Granted, job hunting is hard work, but it's not a prison sentence either. Just as you'd reward an employee for exemplary performance with praise, a bonus, or a gift, treat yourself the same way.

When you achieve a goal, give yourself a treat. I'm not talking about running out and buying a Corvette or flying to Paris for the weekend. A half-day off, a meal in a favorite restaurant, a new dress or tie, theater tickets, or just hanging out with a friend for an evening is what I had in mind. Achievements or major inroads in your job search are relative. A major lead, contact, successful interview, or pending job offer is worthy of reward. You're not impressing anyone by playing the martyr. Uppermost, you're depriving yourself of well-earned self-praise.

Now we're ready to fine-tune some skills and ease the job search into second gear.

YOU ONLY THINK YOU'RE NETWORKING!

I hate the word *networking*. New Age job searchers bat it around as if it were some recently discovered high-tech job-getting strategy. Networking has become another nasty buzzword associated with politically correct job searching. But it's actually a strategy that's been around since Adam pounded the mangroves searching for a job.

Getting beyond the word, networking is the noble art of nurturing and using people as a conduit to jobs, and I heartily endorse it. Not only do masterful networkers get job leads faster than anyone else; they're in the most strategic position to conquer the best ones.

The power brokers, decision makers, and wheeler-dealers of the world are relentless networkers. Prominent politicians, from senators to presidents, have been Olympic-style networkers for years.

I'm not going to insult you by saying that you ought to be networking. You already know that. In some form or fashion, you've been doing it throughout your career. I am going to take you to the next networking level by passing along secrets and insights you may not have considered.

But first, some networking no-nos.

THREE NETWORKING NO-NOS

Maybe 1 out of 100 job searchers networks properly. And that's being generous. At critical points in their career, most job searchers commit the following three no-nos.

1. *Attempting to enlist the help of people you haven't spoken to in years.* Most people network when they lose their jobs. They say to themselves, "I need a job fast so I'd better get on the stick and start

networking." They pull out their address book with names and telephone numbers going all the way back to college and start calling practically everyone they know. "Hi Alice, remember me? We both worked at Elite Graphics 10 years ago. To make a long story short, I've just been canned and I'm looking for a new job. I wondered if you knew anyone looking for an art director with more than 15 years' experience?"

I don't know how you'd react if this person called you, but I know what my first thought would be: "I can't believe she had the chutzpah to call me after 10 years because she thought I could help her find a job!" The upshot is you wouldn't lift a finger to help her. Why should you?

The truth is most people network the way my fictional graphic artist does. Whether it's a distorted sense of their own worth, inflated egos, poor judgment, or just plain old lack of common sense, people make false assumptions about others.

Equally offensive is getting a call from someone you don't know—say, a casual acquaintance of your second cousin—who tells you he's networking to make contacts leading to job interviews. It's one thing to get a call from a distant cousin you see twice a year, but a *friend* of your cousin? That's beyond ridiculous. Appropriate reaction: Hang up the phone and scream, "Spare me the amateurs of the world!"

A working network is made up of strong, well-defined relationships cultivated over time. As the saying goes, there's no such thing as fast friends. Seasoned networkers never ask favors of people with whom they have no relationship. That's the epitome of bad form. Totally uncool.

2. *Aimlessly chatting it up with anyone who crosses your path.* Random kibitzing or schmoozing doesn't equal networking. Productive networkers have a sixth sense about people and leads. Although their every contact doesn't materialize into a potential lead, there's a consistency and theme to their relationships. Ideally, networking is building a universe of people who can help you. George C. Fraser, publisher of *SuccessGuide,* a handbook on African-American career resources, calls networking a "meeting and sharing of mutual opportunities with like-minded businesspeople in a casual and less than formal setting." It's all about building what Fraser calls an "infrastructure of support."

3. *Acting inappropriately intrusive.*   Amateur networkers display an annoying sense of entitlement. They think the world owes them a living. The worst of the lot have a bad attitude on top of it. They're constantly putting both feet in their mouths by pouncing on people at the wrong times. They lack the tact to know when to make their move. They'll call or show up at the most inopportune times, ask ridiculous questions, and hound you to death.

A good example is the 35-year-old advertising copywriter who, during a trade conference, sauntered up to the head of a major advertising agency—just as the executive was in the middle of cementing a megadeal—and said, "Sorry to interrupt, Mr. Steel, but do you remember me? I did a big freelance project for you about 6 months ago...." The copywriter sure made an impression—one that says, "Stay clear of this guy." He's an entrepreneur's worst nightmare.

If the copywriter had thought before he acted, he would have waited for a proper opportunity to corner the agency head alone so he could make a favorable impression.

Creative networking, on the other hand, is like a subtle dance. The best practitioners know when to lead, when to follow, and when just to stand on the sideline waiting for the right moment to make their move. They're lay psychologists who've mastered the art of reading people.

WHO SAID NETWORKING IS A FORMAL PROCESS?

Networking is serious business—anything but a hit-or-miss proposition. It's been proven that clever networking reduces the length of a job search. Supersalesman Harvey Mackay summed up the essence of fruitful networking in his book *Sharkproof:* "It's not who you know and it's not what you know, but what who you know knows." Smart networkers realize this. They also understand that no finite prescription will tell you how to do it correctly. True networking is not a formal process. It's not like following a recipe. Networking is a philosophy and a lifestyle. It's a fluid process or continuum that's always evolving and assuming new shapes and forms. In *How to Find Your Life's Work,* Richard J. Pilder and William F. Pilder define a network as "a structure of relationships through which information and ideas flow in constant motion."

The core of real networking is an unflagging belief that people are ultimately the key to career success. No matter how smart you are, you *can't* do it alone. Knowing that, you always keep your networking antennae up. Successful or on the brink of personal bankruptcy, you're forever networking. It's a way of life.

The unwritten rule of great networking is reciprocity and unselfish sharing of information. Skilled networkers sincerely believe they'll be paid back in some way for a good turn. But accomplished networkers never have their hand out. Ironically, they seldom, if ever, even use the word *networking*. That's because they've woven the art of contact building into the fabric of their lives.

Consider this offbeat example.

Meet Sally D., Virtuoso Networker

Instinctive networker Sally D. hangs out in my old Brooklyn neighborhood. Sally, by the way, is a man, short for Salvatore DeNunzio, Jr. But everyone calls him Sally D. (Brooklynites have a thing for nicknames.) Sally is a hustler and I don't mean that in a negative or, perish the thought, illegal sense. Sally buys and sells anything he can find, from auto parts or clothing to sporting goods and audio equipment.

Because Sally has such great contacts, he's able to buy merchandise directly from manufacturers or wholesalers and turn around and sell it at deep discounts to friends, friends of friends, or anyone else who happens to hear about him. Sally sells his wares from his house or garage. Beyond moving cheap merchandise, he is an incredible information source. The man knows everything that is happening within a 10-mile radius of his home. He can tell you about deals, closeout sales, cheap restaurants, and (yes) who's hiring and firing.

Sally attracts information like a magnet because he's trusted and respected. Tell him something in confidence and torture couldn't pry it from him. Ask him a favor and it's done immediately. Like all great networkers, he never asks anything in return. But in time, he's always paid back with favors, leads, new business, or valuable information. He's what world-class networker Victor Lindquist, former director of Northwestern University's Placement Center, calls a "kingmaker." Sally sits at the hub of the information wheel. News starts with him and filters out to everyone else.

Sally D. is a humble, yet good example of a Class A networker. Within every sector of society—politics, business, or academia—there are kingmaker networkers like him. The most powerful and influential have changed the course of history. Study, befriend, and emulate them. They're well positioned to help you.

The Only Networking Commandment You'll Ever Need

The basic tenet is *everyone is reachable*. Great networkers never say, "Forget about it; nobody can get to her." They'll never eliminate a potentially important contact because she's too powerful, aloof, famous, or rich. Real networkers are unstoppable. They're not intimidated by power, money, or resistance. They know everyone is reachable—from a *Fortune* 500 CEO to the President of the United States. If they're hell-bent on contacting someone, they'll find a way to do so. It may take 12 months, but they stick with it until they "get their man," as the saying goes. Their reasoning is sound. It goes something like this: "We're all in this game of life together to accomplish as much as possible. So give it your best shot and don't let anyone stand in your way."

WHAT GREAT NETWORKERS HAVE IN COMMON

Whether they're in Tibet, Zimbabwe, or Vermont, great networkers have a set of common traits. Follow their lead.

1. *Sincerely like people.*   You can't turn this basic trait on and off like a faucet. If you're a misanthrope, genetically hostile, or simply fear all homo sapiens, pretend to be otherwise and work on it. If you can't do it by yourself, join a support group or find a good therapist. By now you've learned that "team players" go the farthest. Countless surveys rank "interpersonal skills" alongside "ability" as vital assets for career success.

2. *Maintain constant contact.*   There's a point of no return when people cannot be contacted for networking purposes—typically after 3 to 8 years, depending on the nature of the relationship. As with the graphic artist cited earlier, you can't call a college roommate and expect her to help you if you haven't spoken to her in over a decade. Productive networkers stay in touch. Within a 12-month period, they've contacted, either by phone or letter, practically all the people in their network.

3. *Keep an up-to-date log or database.*   Face it. Some people are more organized than others. If you're like me, in a perpetual state of near chaos, you must constantly work at your organization skills. Over the course of your job search, you'll speak to hundreds of people. The only way to stay on top of everyone is by creating some kind of system. If you don't, you'll be randomly calling people in your Rolodex whenever the urge strikes you. That's to be avoided. All it takes is discipline. You can create a file of index cards. Better yet, if you've got a computer, design a networking database. Create a system that's comfortable for you. I've seen all kinds of variations, from simply alphabetizing names to creating specific lists of business, social, and casual contacts. One ambitious job searcher created a list of 400 headhunters across the country. Another uses several lists ranked by importance. The A list, for example, is the blue-chip, hot list of contacts requiring constant attention. The B list logs the runners-up, and the C list contains lukewarm contacts.

Whatever system you create, the idea is to include essential information—name, address, phone number, date of contact, status, and personal observations. Once your system is in place, keep it up to date by constantly adding, deleting, and pruning.

FUNDAMENTALS OF GREAT NETWORKING

You've got the idea. Networking need not be mysterious if you keep the following fundamentals in mind.

1. *Information is priceless; contacts are everywhere.*   An open mind is essential to successful networking. Information and leads are everywhere, sometimes in the most unlikely places. Great networkers know this. They report meeting valuable contacts in airports, on planes or buses, and at popular watering holes. Many career-long relationships have spontaneously started over a beer. You just never know who the man or woman sitting next to you may be. Maybe he's a middle manager like you. Perhaps she's a senior executive in your industry with whom you have many contacts in common. All of a sudden you strike up a conversation, build a rapport, and close with, "Isn't it incredible what a small world it is?" Three hours later, you're entering this person's name in your networking database— maybe on your A list.

2. *The process never stops.* As I mentioned above, successful networking ought to be part of your lifestyle. Whether you are employed or unemployed, it never stops. True networkers never say, "Now that I have a job, the heat's off. I can ease up on the reins." More likely, they'll go at it more aggressively, thinking, "Now that I'm well positioned in a good company, I can make some incredible contacts."

Uppermost, networking is never considered work. Networkers and game hunters have a lot in common. Never knowing what lies around the bend, they love the challenge and excitement of the hunt.

3. *One good turn deserves another.* It's the unwritten code of honor underlying great networking: "If you get me a great account, job candidate, stock tip, or valuable information, you'll be paid back handsomely." The payback is not going to be out of a sense of duty, but rather because of heartfelt gratitude and loyalty. There's that special human equation that's the leitmotif of great networking.

CHECK OUT FORMAL NETWORKING GROUPS

Just as there are support groups for job hunters, so formal groups have been established for networkers. Some are excellent; others are little more than social clubs. If it's just a hodgepodge of job searchers from many fields and age groups all looking for contacts, leads, and information, why bother? For example, many YMCAs, YMHAs, churches, and synagogues offer freewheeling networking groups. Approach them with caution, expecting little. If you're lucky, you might make a valuable connection.

Check out more fruitful formal avenues that could open doors. Your local Forty Plus chapter, for example, may schedule meetings of professionals in your industry. Also, many organizations create planned networking opportunities. Engineering societies do this all the time.

Over the past half-decade, more and more colleges and universities have been offering alumni networking services. Although many of these groups are made up of younger alums, who's to say your school hasn't created a special group for older graduating classes? It's a chance to see old cronies and cement old relationships—or maybe build some new ones. What do you have to lose?

Many of the larger schools around the country offer sophisticated networking opportunities. Cornell University in Ithaca, NY, offers networking opportunities in Boston, New York, Philadelphia, Chicago, San Francisco, and Los Angeles. The American Graduate School of International Management, popularly known as Thunderbird, in Phoenix, AZ, presents a unique networking opportunity called "First Tuesday." On the first Tuesday of every month, 22,000 alums of Thunderbird, the largest graduate business school in the United States, meet to network at designated spots, usually favorite watering holes or restaurants, in every major city in the country.

Don't stop there. Put your investigator's hat on and look for nonprofit and government organizations that offer networking opportunities. Certainly, the local chamber of commerce may be able to help you. You also may be pleasantly surprised at what you'll find in the Yellow Pages under the general employment heading. The Older Women's League, a national grassroots advocacy organization dedicated to improving the status of women's lives, offers networking groups in some of its 80 chapters throughout the United States. Call its toll-free number (800-825-3695) to find out if anything is cooking near you.

Finally, look at profit-making businesses that sell networking services. For example, Exec-U-Net, based in Norwalk, CT, has five locations throughout the country. Its 2000 members pay annual dues of $260 to receive an exclusive 20-page newsletter offering about 150 job leads. Executive Director David Opton swears the leads come from a number of exclusive sources, such as executive search firms. He insists that none of the jobs has been advertised and that 7 out of 10 executives who change jobs do so through networking opportunities. He's also biased because it's his company. But you have nothing to lose by calling to find out more.

Let's press on and find out what companies are looking for.

WHAT ARE COMPANIES LOOKING FOR?

It's the million-dollar question with some surprising answers. Don't ever believe anyone who tells you that employers always look for the same qualifications. The truth is, everything changes—people, economies, and job markets. It's just a question of when and how. Any organization paying someone to do a job wants to get its money's worth. That's an obvious given in any age. But the kind of person employers want and the nature of the work relationship have radically changed over the past half-century. It will continue to evolve as we rocket toward the millennium.

As I said earlier, the problem is that many 50-plus job searchers spent most of their careers in an unrealistic twilight zone working for one company. After nearly a decade of rampant downsizing, it's hard to fathom such a world. One day the walls came tumbling down and corporate America's gatekeepers delivered bad news. The company was in Chapter 11 or it had merged or consolidated. Departments were cut or eliminated and middle-management ranks were slashed. For your devoted efforts and loyalty, you got a cryptic memo you didn't really understand, along with a handshake, pat on the back, severance package, pension, and timetable for clearing off your desk and getting the hell out. In short, your services were no longer needed. You made a beeline to your favorite watering hole and thought to yourself, "How's that for gratitude?"

It marked the end of a lifestyle and the beginning of a new chapter in your life. Like it or not, you were left having to wheel-and-deal in a high-energy job market that insisted upon perfection—whatever that meant. Employers' new hiring motto was, "Get the job done right with as few people as possible, and make no long-term promises." Repressed button-down human resources types call it "maximizing human resources." In plain English, hire people willing to work their butts off.

The next time you hear about "cradle-to-retirement job security," you'll be watching a nostalgic documentary on the 1950s.

NOBODY IS WAITING FOR YOU

Get humble fast and see the new world as it is. The cold truth is, no one is waiting for you. And I'm not blaming the age issue either. It's a buyer's market, a point I'll drive home as often as I can. Employers' new hiring attitude is, "Impress me, I dare you!" Why shouldn't they feel that way? Heck, if you were running a company and staying up nights figuring out how to remain profitable and fend off the competition nibbling at your market, you'd want the best talent you could find too. Hiring the wrong person is not only a waste of money; it could slow you down. That spells potential death in the entrepreneurial race for market dominance.

Leave nothing to the imagination. Impress employers by doing a compelling show-stopping tap dance that drives home your talents with the fervor of a streetcorner evangelist. You must be a super-salesperson who doesn't know the meaning of the word *no*. You must have the ego of a politician combined with the humility of a monk. Qualifications are great, but it's your ability to sell them to an employer that's going to get you a job.

GIVE ME PEOPLE WHO CAN HIT THE GROUND RUNNING

Understand the realities of the career world and you'll be ready to pitch yourself accordingly. The goal is convincing employers you're not a vestige of a bygone work era, but a high-energy chameleon who quickly adapts to any environment. Picture yourself walking out a revolving door and walking back in with a new attitude and take on life. Here's what companies are looking for.

Recyclable Workers

Just as you'd recalibrate, redesign, or rebuild a machine to produce new and improved widgets, companies want workers who can wear many hats. Employers want to know you can spin on a dime to do whatever is demanded of you. Say your marketing manager unexpectedly jumps ship for a bigger and better job. Well, now you're a marketing person until a replacement is found. Your boss suddenly has to fly cross-country to sell a potential client. You must take the helm and steer the ship. That means opening the business at 7:30 a.m. and working till 9:00 p.m. Instead of balking at the increased workload, you jump at the chance to strut your stuff. So what if it means canceling some dinner appointments or a planned vacation? Specialty workers of the 1960s and 1970s have been replaced by high-powered multiskilled generalists. These are roll-up-your-sleeves types who can knock out a letter on a dinosaur manual typewriter or cruise cyberspace like a veteran hacker searching the globe for the best price of rolled steel.

Clutch Players

It's a new philosophy toward hiring. Companies have discovered creative ways not to make long-term commitments. The new thinking is, "Why put anyone on the payroll if we don't have to—or unless we have no choice." Hence, the term *just-in-time hiring*. In the past, companies stockpiled workers. They hired more than they actually needed so work could be spread out. Now, it's wait until the critical last moment and hire a *Terminator* clone who can do the work of a dozen people. Other employers are opting for short-term relationships, which are either project-based or contractual arrangements.

It's as simple as hiring people for a clearly defined task (a marketing research project or an advertising campaign, for example) and then showing them the door when they're finished. Cyclical and seasonal companies do this all the time. Clothing and toy manufacturers and department stores require more bodies around the busy Christmas season to make, package, ship, and sell their goods. If they are lucky, at the end of the season, these people will be reassigned to other areas where their skills can be tapped.

Don't be put off by the temporary nature of the work. There are no guarantees and you could be back on the street in 3 months. But it's also an opportunity to learn and make contacts. Even if it doesn't materialize into a long-term job, you're ahead of the game because you have more skills to market.

Job Hoppers

Remember when job hoppers were considered rootless, itinerant screw-ups who couldn't hold down a job if their life depended upon it? The prejudice against job hoppers was part of the old work ethic: Companies searched for stalwart workers who had only two or three jobs throughout their entire career. Need I remind you about Big Blue and a slew of other two-faced *Fortune* 500 companies that promoted the concept of lifetime employment and then abandoned it when the going got rough? What they withheld from their troops until the last grueling minute was that profits were more important than people. But give them a big round of applause for removing the stigma against job hopping—the survival tactic of the future.

PACKAGE YOUR EXPERIENCE

Don't apologize because you've had five jobs over the last 15 years. See it as a strong selling point. Tie the experiences together to make a compelling case for your consideration. The point is to make each job into an opportunity to learn and grow. Each one took you farther along the vast career highway. Security isn't the thing; it's improvement and self-fulfillment. In other words, you're a better person for each job. Even career changers can take this tack by finding a common skill to sell from two totally different industries.

A social worker turned stockbroker did this successfully when he convinced a well-known nationwide brokerage house to hire him. Yes, social work and selling stocks are oceans apart, yet they both require a critical skill—understanding and communicating with people. When he made this point during his interview and went on to say he was convinced he'd make an excellent broker because of his social work experience, the interviewer took a deep breath, paused 30 seconds, and agreed with him. A week later, he was hired. There are hundreds of inspiring stories just like his. If you're like me, a veteran job hopper and proud of it, you've been liberated.

A recommended exercise is making a list of all the jobs you've had and then writing out the good and bad points of each one. Uppermost, jot down what you learned from each. The painless exercise will help you sell yourself better when you are asked about prior jobs.

Now you're ready to explore some job avenues you've never considered—or even known about.

HIDDEN MARKET GEMS NO ONE TALKS ABOUT

You've read so much about the hidden job market, you're probably bored to tears at the mere mention of the term. You already know that most available jobs, maybe 75 to 80 percent of them, can be found there. Big deal!

But I guarantee you've never considered the hidden market avenues I'm about to share. The majority of career writers obsess over the fact that the published market—want ads posted by companies and employment agencies—is an unproductive route to take because you're fighting a numbers game. Career heavies advise job searchers to be creative, yet fail to point out actual hidden market opportunities. Finding them is like striking gold. First you discover a deposit with a hint of gold that, when traced, leads to a big find. It's the same way with the hidden market. Once you stumble on one lead, others follow.

Let's start with organizations.

LOCAL AND NATIONAL JOB-FINDING ORGANIZATIONS

Just as you searched the Yellow Pages for potential networking organizations, so you should use them to locate organizations in the job-finding business. Plenty exist to serve different markets. Here are three to consider.

National Executive Service Corps (NESC); Senior Career Planning and Placement Service (SCPPS). NESC offers management consulting services to nonprofit organizations operating in 41 cities. SCPPS is its placement service for downsized and retired executives who are looking for second careers. Operating like an inexpensive executive recruiting firm, it charges applicants a $500 fee and 20 percent of their first year's salary. Based in New York, SCPPS services nonprofit organizations throughout the country. Companies with short-term projects are finding that it makes more sense to hire a seasoned executive than untested part-time help or an expensive independent consultant. For information, write the National Executive Service Corps, 257 Park Ave. South, New York, NY 10010-7304. Or call (212) 529-6660.

Operation ABLE (Ability Based on Long Experience).   A nonprofit organization, ABLE helps older job searchers find full-time, part-time, and temporary jobs. ABLE also provides career counseling, testing, and assessment services that often lead to training or retraining for job seekers. The government, foundations, and individual contributors pay for ABLE's programs. Services are free to job searchers. The original ABLE operation began in Chicago and was the model for nine others nationwide. They are:

1. Rainier Job Service Center/Experience Plus, Chicago
2. Older Workers Employment Council, Denver Metropolitan Area
3. Operation ABLE of Southeast Nebraska
4. Operation ABLE of Michigan
5. Vermont Associates for Training and Development, Inc.
6. Operation ABLE of Greater Boston
7. ABLE Senior Employment Services, New York
8. Atlanta Regional Commission
9. Arkansas ABLE
10. Career Encore, Los Angeles

For information about the ABLE network, write to Operation ABLE, 180 N. Wabash Ave., Suite 802, Chicago, IL 60601.

American Association of Retired Persons (AARP).   With more than 33 million members, AARP wields a lot of clout. Its magazine, *Modern Maturity,* boasts a circulation of over 20 million. Put it all together and you have a powerful organization providing its members with a raft of services that range from medical insurance and travel discounts to job information. If you're not a member, I urge you to join. Dues are cheap. More important, it pays to plug into the AARP network to keep abreast of events and programs of interest. It's also a good idea to call your local AARP chapter to find out about programs for job hunters.

Two years ago, for example, AARP launched the Job Hub in New York City, a unique service providing local businesses with a talent pool of workers from assorted backgrounds, including secretaries, computer operators, word processors, clerks, receptionists, office service personnel, accountants, salespeople, managers, entrepreneurs, and professionals from many fields. Applicants are prescreened by AARP volunteers and come from area universities and city agencies that include Aging in America, YWCA (New York City), Department for the Aging, and New York Foundation for Senior Citizens.

It pays to be part of such a labor pool. A local employer may be looking for your special talents. Over the next couple of years, Job Hubs will be starting up in other cities.

GOVERNMENT-SPONSORED PROGRAMS

If you've got no patience for bureaucracy and all the inescapable red tape, procedures, and annoying paperwork that accompany it, you'll have problems dealing with government agencies. That's a fact of life that'll never change. Nevertheless, government agencies at both federal and state levels offer several services for older job searchers. In fact, additional programs will be kicking off over the next few years. So take a deep breath and get ready to experience megadoses of frustration. It's worth it for a pearl of a job lead.

At the federal level, programs are sponsored by the Division of Older Worker Programs (U.S. Department of Labor's Employment and Training Administration). Started in 1965 under Title 5 of the Older Americans Act, the program administers grants to 10 national nonprofit organizations and state agencies, as determined by Congress. The American Association of Retired People (AARP), for example, is a grantee. A program specialist can tell you about the grantees near you. Once you pass the eligibility requirements, interviews, and physical examination, you're placed in a community service organization (hospital, nursing home, public school, YMCA).

Approximately 20 percent of the enrollees move into profit-making or government organizations. More than 30,000 people go through the program every year. The best part is it costs nothing.

Regionally, each state sponsors its own programs. Call your state's department of labor to find out what programs it offers for older workers. New York, for example, operates the Worker Opportunity and Reemployment Center, offering training opportunities, tuition assistance, a placement service, and fax machines and computers for job hunters to develop their own materials. Even though it's available to all workers over 18, more than 25 percent of applicants are over 55.

OFF-THE-BEATEN-TRACK LEADS

Business Incubators

You don't have to be a detective to know that emerging businesses breed jobs. And business incubators are just one place to find them.

An *incubator* is an apparatus for the maintenance of controlled conditions. In hospitals, it's a warm environment allowing premature babies to grow until strong enough to thrive on their own. Not dissimilar, business incubators provide start-up companies with a controlled, nurturing environment in which to flourish. Housing several developing businesses under one roof, incubators range from 10,000 square feet to more than 400,000 square feet. The largest incubator houses 77 tenants; the median number is about 8.

Incubators serve practically all nonretail industries, with a concentration on high-technology and light manufacturing. They're run by nonprofit organizations (universities and colleges), profit-making businesses, economic development agencies, and local governments.

The incubator acts as a mother hen to fledgling businesses, providing such critical business services as below-market rates, shared business operations (telephone answering, bookkeeping, word processing, and secretarial help), business and technical assistance (legal, accounting, and marketing advice), and financial assistance (advice for securing bank or venture capital aid).

If you're looking for creative new businesses, incubators are the place to find them. They're ideal for inventors, for example. An inventor's biggest problem is finding people who'll offer the right advice without charging exorbitant fees.

Companies starting out in incubators are lean operations, often employing just a handful of people. Because of their carefully nurtured beginnings, they grow rapidly. Within a few years, a 3- to 5-person operation will expand into a 35- to 40-person organization. Development Strategies Corporation, a market analysis company in Gloucester, MA, reports that businesses launched in incubators stand a much better chance of survival than traditional start-ups. About 50 to 75 percent of all businesses fail within the first 3 years, yet only 10 to 20 percent of companies nurtured in incubators die within the first 5 years.

The good news is that the incubator industry is relatively new and just taking off. About 500 business incubators house more than 6000 tenants throughout the United States, up from only 15 in 1980. New incubators are opening at the rate of 4 to 5 a month. By the year 2000, there'll be over 1000 incubators in the United States. Take the hint: Incubator companies need experienced people willing to roll up their sleeves and pitch in.

Finding Incubators.   You may be pleasantly surprised to discover a couple of incubators in your own backyard. Here are three organizations that can point you to them.

> *National Business Incubation Association* (1 President St., Athens, OH 45701; 614-593-4331). NBIA is a membership association of more than 500 small business incubators.
>
> *U.S. Small Business Administration (SBA): Office of Private Sector Initiatives* (1441 L St. NW, Suite 720A, Washington, DC 20416; 202-205-6730). This national clearinghouse on small business incubators maintains a database of incubator projects throughout the country.
>
> *Corporation for Enterprise Development* (777 N. Capitol St. NE, Suite 801, Washington, DC 20002; 202-408-9788). CFED is a nonprofit organization that studies and promotes economic development for low-income communities.

Making Contact.   The guardian of the gate is the incubator manager. Incubators are run by managers who also double as business counselors. They can tell you everything you need to know: kinds of tenants, how long they've been there, what stage the business is in, and most critical, which job prospects are the most fertile. Make a great impression. Get on their wrong side and you don't stand a prayer.

High-potential incubators are fertile business investments. It's something to keep in mind if you're sitting on a hefty severance package. More than just a great job, an incubator could also be an exciting investment. Be careful. First, you have to have an entrepreneurial gene dormant somewhere. As soon as you become a business partner, you've elevated your job to a 7-day-a-week obsession. Second, be sure to research the company thoroughly and get solid advice from a battle-worn attorney and accountant.

Research Parks

Run by universities throughout the United States, research parks are a sophisticated relative of incubators. Rather than housing different companies in one building, research parks are aligned with technologies that the university is developing. Whereas incubators nurture start-up companies, research parks house mostly mid-size and large companies, according to the Association of University-Related Research Parks, a central clearinghouse for information on planning, construction, marketing, and management of university research parks. Research park companies can take advantage of the university's facilities, faculty, and student body. Approximately 210,000 people work for 2800 companies located in research parks.

A Coopers & Lybrand study reported that the typical university-related research park has two buildings with 211,000 gross square feet, 12 tenant companies with 300 total employees, and a $250,000 operating budget—all on a 200-acre site.

Making Contact.   Check out local universities to find out if they house research parks. Then call the park manager, the equivalent of the incubator manager. Ask all the right questions and, if you're lucky, you'll walk away with some exciting leads.

Enterprise Zones

If you think incubators and research parks are far out, wait till you hear about enterprise zones. They were started in the early 1980s to combat poverty and restore depressed areas by offering tax breaks and other government incentives to attract entrepreneurs with a frontier mentality. Still in the development phase, they've been the subject of heated controversy. Opponents argue that instead of creating business opportunities for residents of depressed areas, enterprise zones attract outsiders who exploit tax savings. Supporters praise enterprise zones as vibrant tools for turning around decaying areas.

Getting beyond the politics, enterprise zones create jobs. If you've got a sense of adventure, you ought to check them out. But keep in mind that many of these neighborhoods are high-crime areas.

Approximately 32 states have enacted enterprise zone legislation. Each state insists that candidate zones meet certain economic distress requirements, such as high unemployment, population loss, or a high level of low-income residents. About 4700 businesses are located within the zones, employing anywhere from 6 workers to more than 200 staffers. The U.S. Small Business Administration (SBA) reports that companies with fewer than 100 employees are the most important sources of job growth in enterprise zones.

Finding Enterprise Zones.   Your local economic development organization can tell you if any zones are near you. You'll be amazed at how different they are. Some are no bigger than a local neighborhood; others embrace a sizable chunk of a city. The Louisville, KY enterprise zone, for example, spans over 45 miles—that's twice the size of Newark, NJ.

Find out the objectives of the zone and the kinds of businesses located there. Most zones have similar objectives to encourage business activity and create new jobs for area residents. However, if the types of companies don't interest you, don't pursue this avenue.

SMALL BUSINESS DEVELOPMENT CENTERS

A safer bet is the small business development center (SBDC). SBDCs are easy to find and plenty exist. Supervised by the SBA, the SBDC program offers management assistance to established and new business owners.

There are 55 small business development centers—one or more in each of the 50 states, the District of Columbia, Puerto Rico, and the Virgin Islands—with a network of more than 700 branch locations. A "lead" organization sponsors the SBDC and manages each program. The lead organization coordinates program services at sub-centers and satellite locations at colleges, universities, community colleges, vocational schools, chambers of commerce, and economic development corporations.

SBDCs are hotbeds of entrepreneurial activity; hence, they're a good place to uncover job leads. All it takes is some nosing around. An information-hungry entrepreneur who could welcome your assistance might be tapping an SBDC center near you right now.

Your mission is to find out who's using SBDC services. The best person to give you that information is the SBDC director. Rather than cold-calling, prepare a candid letter briefly outlining your qualifications and explaining that you're looking for potential job leads. Ask for an appointment or, the next best thing, for the director to pass your letter on to entrepreneurs who might be interested. Follow up in 6 to 8 days with a phone call and hope for the best.

Below are the locations of the 55 SBDCs.

1. University of Alaska, Anchorage, AK (907) 274-7232
2. University of Alabama, Birmingham, AL (205) 934-7260
3. University of Arkansas, Little Rock, AR (501) 324-9043
4. Western International University, Phoenix, AZ (602) 943-2311
5. Department of Commerce, Sacramento, CA (916) 324-5068
6. Office of Business Development, Denver, CO (303) 892-3809
7. University of Connecticut, Storrs, CT (203) 486-4135
8. Howard University, Washington, DC (202) 806-1550
9. University of Delaware, Newark, DE (302) 831-2747
10. University of Georgia, Athens, GA (404) 542-5760
11. University of Hawaii, Hilo, HI (808) 933-3515
12. Iowa State University, Ames, IA (515) 292-6351
13. Boise State University, Boise, ID (208) 385-1640
14. Department of Commerce and Community Affairs, Springfield, IL (217) 524-5856
15. Economic Development Council, Indianapolis, IN (317) 264-6871
16. Wichita State University, Wichita, KS (316) 689-3193

17. University of Kentucky, Lexington, KY (606) 257-7668
18. Northeast Louisiana University, Monroe, LA (318) 342-5506
19. University of Massachusetts, Amherst, MA (413) 545-6301
20. Department of Economic and Employment Development, Baltimore, MD (301) 333-6996
21. University of Southern Maine, Portland, ME (207) 780-4420
22. Wayne State University, Detroit, MI (313) 577-4848
23. Department of Trade and Economic Development, St. Paul, MN (612) 297-5770
24. University of Missouri, Columbia, MO (314) 882-0344
25. University of Mississippi, University, MS (601) 232-5001
26. Department of Commerce, Helena, MT (406) 444-4780
27. University of North Carolina, Raleigh, NC (919) 571-4154
28. University of North Dakota, Grand Forks, ND (701) 777-3700
29. University of Nebraska, Omaha, NE (402) 554-2521
30. University of New Hampshire, Durham, NH (603) 862-2200
31. Rutgers University, Newark, NJ (201) 648-5950
32. Santa Fe Community College, Santa Fe, NM (505) 438-1362
33. University of Nevada, Reno, NV (702) 784-1717
34. State University of New York, Albany, NY (2 locations) (518) 443-5398
35. Department of Development, Columbus, OH (614) 466-2711
36. S.E. Oklahoma State University, Durant, OK (405) 924-0277
37. Lane Community College, Eugene, OR (503) 726-2250
38. University of Pennsylvania, Philadelphia, PA (215) 898-1219
39. University of Puerto Rico, Mayaguez, PR (809) 834-3590
40. Bryant College, Springfield, RI (401) 232-6111
41. University of South Carolina, Columbia, SC (803) 777-4907
42. University of South Dakota, Vermillion, SD (605) 677-5272
43. Memphis State University, Memphis, TN (901) 678-2500
44. Dallas Community College, Dallas, TX (214) 565-5833
45. University of Houston, Houston, TX (713) 753-8444
46. Texas Tech University, Lubbock, TX (806) 745-3973

47. University of Texas, San Antonio, TX (512) 224-0791
48. University of Utah, Salt Lake City, UT (801) 581-7905
49. Department of Economic Development, Richmond, VA (804) 371-8258
50. University of Vermont, Williston, VT (802) 878-0181
51. University of the Virgin Islands, St. Thomas, USVI (809) 776-3206
52. Washington State University, Pullman, WA (509) 335-1576
53. University of Wisconsin, Madison, WI (608) 263-7794
54. Governor's Office of Community and Industrial Development, Charleston, WV (304) 558-2960
55. Casper Community College, Casper, WY (307) 235-4825

ENTREPRENEURIAL CENTERS

Another seldom-pursued job avenue is the entrepreneurial center. Teaching entrepreneurialism—the dos, don'ts, and strategies of launching and managing a business—has become very popular over the last decade. As companies continue to shed their human cargo, nearly 300 colleges have started teaching some variation of the entrepreneurial curriculum that includes courses, lectures, seminars, workshops, and degree programs. The University of Southern California (USC) boasts a comprehensive entrepreneurial program that started in 1971. Harvard, Wharton, Wichita State, St. Louis University, University of Arizona, Indiana University, and New York University, to name a few, offer well-rounded entrepreneurial programs.

Here's a ready-made opportunity to hook up with entrepreneurs who are either taking or giving courses. Many take courses to firm up their business acts; others give them for exposure, credibility, and ego stroking. No matter how you size up the situation, entrepreneurial centers present fertile networking opportunities for entrepreneurs and job seekers alike.

The person to befriend is the director of the entrepreneurial program. Typically, program directors are outgoing entrepreneurial types themselves who'll probably admire your clever job-pursuing tactic. They're also seasoned networkers plugged into the entire business community. Beyond knowing who's giving and taking courses, they're aware of who the winners and losers are and can point you to the superstars in the wings. The program director is a wealth of information. Take advantage of the opportunity to uncover such leads.

Again, a terse professional letter is the way to open the door. Then schedule an appointment and tell your story. You stand an excellent chance of walking away with valuable information.

TRADE OR PROFESSIONAL ASSOCIATIONS AND INDUSTRY RAGS

Name any field or profession and I guarantee there are maybe two, possibly a handful of trade or professional associations serving it. All industry associations are not the same. The big, well-funded ones have more power and, naturally, are better information resources. Some have thousands of members spread across the United States, whereas small regional ones may have a few hundred. Either type, however, can be useful if you make valuable connections. The irrefutable logic is you're bound to pick up job leads from people in your industry. The more contacts you have, the better the odds of capturing exclusive information. You don't have to go to every association meeting and event. The idea is to be plugged in and know what's happening. Find the wheeler-dealers and stay in touch.

A great source for locating all the associations serving your field is the *Encyclopedia of Associations* (Gale Research), which most libraries stock. I guarantee you'll uncover industry associations you've never heard of before. New organizations in virtually all industries are starting up every day.

Finally, stay on top of industry publications as well. Like trade organizations, some carry more clout than others. The sheer size of a publication tells you a lot. Many are gorged with news, events, opinions, and (yes), job listings. Even if trade mags carry no job listings, it pays to skim them to stay on top of trends.

GETTING ON A HEADHUNTER'S GOOD SIDE

I don't have to tell you what headhunters do. You already know they're valuable. And like most seasoned professionals, you're probably intimidated by them—for good reason. Face it. They're not called headhunters for nothing. Many are ruthless egotists, power brokers who'd ransom their parents for priceless job leads. Others are ethical professionals. Yet most act and think like high-ranking dignitaries. They like to be catered to, stroked, and above all respected. After all, *headhunter* is not the most flattering term. The best of them thrive on the chase, mining and hunting for the right body to claim a whopping 33.3 percent of a candidate's first-year salary.

No wonder they're impossible to reach. Their theme song is "Don't call us, we'll call you." They mean it too. Nevertheless, search firms aren't unapproachable. Nothing is impossible, not even reaching prima donna headhunters.

If you've mastered the art of working with them, the rewards can be priceless. First, you'll be considered if you match the qualifications of a search on which they're working. Second, they're an incredible information resource. The average search firm has AAA-rated information from key decision makers, running the gamut from trends and salary ranges to the types of information technology used by the leading firms. Once you've established a relationship, they'll share information with you. The more you know, the easier you are to sell.

Hundreds of headhunting firms are scattered across the United States. Confine yourself to a select list that can help you. The best source for a listing of search firms is Jim Kennedy's *Directory of Executive Recruiters* (Templeton Road, Fitzwilliam, NH 03447). It's updated yearly, listing recruiters alphabetically by industry, job function, and geography.

The trick is working your way into the headhunters' network. Here's how to do so.

1. *Jump when they call.*   Search professionals enjoy their power. Some gloat in it. Most pull down six-figure salaries; the superstars are in the rarefied seven-figure zone. They thrive on running the show and wielding enormous power. You either play by their rules or you don't play at all. When they call, they expect you to jump. If summoned, don't set conditions or stipulations. Just say, "When, where, and I'll be there." Don't worry about expense. They'll cover all your costs. Money is no object, since they pay for nothing. All expenses are picked up by the client.

Some recruiters have a penchant for meeting applicants in airports. I've heard countless stories of applicants flying cross-country for a 20-minute meeting with a recruiter. Other recruiters prefer scheduling early-morning, prebreakfast meetings, and still others relish screening applicants in the back of a limo. Be loose. Whatever the circumstances of the meeting, go with it. Be thankful you were deemed worthy of their priceless time.

2. *Don't be a pest.*   Let them discover you. Don't ask for a meeting. Even if you've got incredible credentials, there is no reason for them to call you if they don't have a position you match. Use a little psychology. Successful headhunters love what they do. Along with big bucks and the fast-track lifestyle, they relish the thrill of the chase. So just discovering the talent to match a search is a real high for these folks.

3. *Stay in touch.*   The trick to being discovered is staying in touch. The only way to do that is to write headhunters constantly so your credentials are implanted in their brains. Chances are they won't even acknowledge receipt of your letters. But that doesn't mean you've been forgotten. Present yourself well on paper and you'll be put in their database. Guaranteed, your name will come up during the next database search for someone with your experience.

The best way to make a headhunter's database is not by forwarding a résumé with a perfunctory cover letter, but by sending a terse summary letter describing yourself. (I'll get into the big topic of why letters are more powerful selling tools than résumés later.) The brief letter to headhunters should contain the following critical information:

- Straightforward explanation of who you are and the kind of position you want
- Description of your qualifications
- List of your most recent employers, including dates and position titles

It only sounds simple. You'll soon see that capturing yourself in a few paragraphs isn't easy. You're not including all your qualifications and every job you've ever had, just the *selling highlights*. So give it time and thought. If there is a change in your status—for instance, you've conquered a new assignment or project, even if it's short-term—keep headhunters informed.

Rest assured, when headhunters want you, they'll find you. They're not beyond calling you at home at 1 a.m. if they think you're right for a search. Once you've made the grade and are in a headhunter's good graces, you won't be forgotten. Your patience and professionalism will pay off.

Let's shift gears and check out the information highway for job leads.

CRUISING CYBERSPACE FOR JOB LEADS

It's okay to reminisce about the good old days. It's even okay to tell close friends how much you prefer banging out letters and memos on your clunky old manual typewriter. But don't ever confess that to a potential employer. You'll be whisked to the door so fast your head will spin. Not only must you be open to new technologies, you'd better be adept at using them. Like the workplace, the job mart has been electronically revolutionized.

LEARN THE LINGO

Get with the program. The hot high-tech topic these days is the *Internet*, the global web of computer information networks. If you can't cruise cyberspace on the Internet—an electronic behemoth spawning businesses and controversy at the same time—you're out of touch, a Neanderthal in the space age.

The Internet took shape about a decade ago as a data link for elite academic communities. The sprawling network links more than 2.2 million computers on 32,400 networks and is accessible in 135 countries. It's estimated that over 25 million people have the capability of sending electronic mail messages on the Internet.

Now the Internet has been commandeered by the business world. It's safe to say the number of commercial computers linked directly to the Internet has surpassed the number of Net host computers in the academic world.

The growth is awesome. Each month, dozens of companies are starting to offer related services to businesses and individuals. According to one source, the Internet represents a $10-billion-a-year business. Overstated or not, one thing is certain: Internet is a powerful communications tool. It's open 24 hours a day and is global in reach. The Net has joined the ranks of the telephone, telex, and fax machine as an essential communications vehicle.

If people tell you they're Net surfers, it doesn't mean they've been catching some waves; it means they can sprint around the Internet with the agility of trained runners. In short, the Net translates to another job-hunting avenue.

ON-LINE SERVICES FOR JOB SEARCHERS

Over the past 18 months, several national on-line employment advertising services have been created. For little or no fee, many of them permit job hunters to search through listings of about 5000 professional openings and include their résumés in databanks. A number of commercial on-line services are also offering specialized bulletin boards, permitting job hunters to use electronic mail to post their résumés into a database and respond to job announcements.

Before investigating commercial on-line job-hunting services, check out the free ones first. Most states provide job banks through the 2000-plus state employment services scattered across the 50 states. State governments may be overwhelming bureaucracies, but they're also a wealth of career information. All states are federally funded to operate a labor exchange or employment service, free to employers and job applicants. Along with traditional career services for over-50 job searchers, most states offer easy-to-use on-line job listings. All you have to do is sit in front of a personal computer and hone in on jobs that interest you by moving through a series of occupational categories. Check your telephone book to find the nearest state employment service.

Now for a few popular commercial on-line services.

CompuServe Information Service (P.O. Box 20212, Columbus, OH 43220; 800-848-8199). CompuServe boasts an on-line "headhunting" service, a fast, inexpensive way to find bodies without contending with employment agencies or executive recruiters. Your qualifications are available on-line to hundreds of *Fortune* 500 companies and start-up companies. If a human resources person thinks you fit a job description, you'll be summoned for an interview. CompuServe reports 100 new companies log on each week.

America On-Line, Inc. (8619 Westwood Center Drive, Vienna, VA 22182; 800-827-6364). Offering databases for job searchers and entrepreneurs, its popular "Career Center" database is updated weekly. The database contains 4000 jobs throughout the United States, accessible 24 hours a day. Creator Jim Gonyea swears it's the first electronic career guidance and employment center in the United States. His "Occupational Profiles" database details more than 700 occupations, along with information about specific companies, working conditions, job outlook, and salary ranges.

Peterson's Guides (P.O. Box 2123 Carnegie Center, Princeton, NJ 08543; 800-338-3282). The folks who publish college guides and career books also offer the on-line service "Connexion," a variation of the above services. Applicants' qualifications are made available to over 200 companies and executive recruiters across the United States.

DON'T PUT ALL YOUR EGGS IN ONE BASKET

Traveling the information superhighway for job leads adds a whole new dimension to job hunting. It's fun and novel, but don't be sucked into the obvious trap and think all this information is exclusive. Many of the job listings are out of date. Some job searchers complain that a significant percentage of jobs have already been filled. America On-Line's creator, Jim Gonyea, admitted that many of his job listings originally appeared as paid ads elsewhere. His service just changed the wording and posted them. It doesn't sound kosher, but copyright attorneys say the practice is perfectly legal as long as on-line services don't use the same language as that of the original ad.

Finally, posting applicant applications on-line doesn't mean prospective employers will read them.

See on-line services for what they are: another potential job source, no better or worse than any other. Like anything new, they're surrounded by hype. In a few years, there's a good chance career experts will compare them to newspaper want ads and advise avoiding them because the odds of capturing an employer's attention are so high.

Advice: No matter how formidable the odds, pursue all job leads. You just may score.

WAIT AND SEE

At the moment, cyberspace is a vast, uncharted, and unregulated frontier that everyone is trying to explore. It's reminiscent of the migration to the American West in search of gold at the turn of the twentieth century. But stay tuned. The best is yet to come. Right now, there is a glut of services on the Internet. Expect a shakeout over the next half-decade. Many services will fall by the wayside, with stronger, more resilient ones replacing them.

More than another job avenue, see cyberspace as a vast information resource. It's also a fertile source of news, trends, company information, and statistics. More and more companies, for example, will be using the Internet as an advertising vehicle.

Keep on cruising the Net. You never know when you'll stumble on an information gem.

THINK SMALL!

Big doesn't mean better. A fast-track career once meant working for a household-name conglomerate with tentacles encircling the globe. It was an impressive status symbol, a hallmark of success. That myth was shattered during the 1980s. If you want proof, ask the thousands of refugees from big-name companies who are out there looking for jobs. I already blew up the fantasy of finding lifetime security in a large company. Let's go one step further and discover where fertile job opportunities can be found.

You don't have to be an economist to know that big companies are not the job generators they were a decade ago. Most career experts insist the best opportunities can be found in small companies. Yet a vocal minority argue that big companies are still fertile career grounds and small companies are not all they're cracked up to be. They cite a study which found that companies with at least 10 workers created nearly two-thirds of all new manufacturing jobs from 1973 to 1988. However, the study also pointed out that small companies similarly eliminate jobs at a far higher rate. What's more, their job cuts are not as visible because layoffs by a big company make national headlines, whereas the disappearance of a tiny company is hardly noticed.

Who's right?

SMALL ENTREPRENEURS ARE THE REAL JOB GENERATORS

It's time to set the record straight. Big companies are still hiring; however, they're hiring fewer workers than they did in the past and doing so very selectively. Face it. Despite what the human resources folks tell you, if you're over 45, have experience, and earned a hefty salary on your last job, the unspoken credo is: "Find someone younger and cheaper."

According to the U.S. Bureau of Labor Statistics, by the year 2000 employment in *Fortune* 500 companies will be halved to 8 million, down from 16 million in 1980. And even though many large companies have reorganized into self-governing divisions to improve efficiency, others are still in for hard times. They're in the process of cutting back, with more layoffs planned.

For those reasons alone, you'd do better pursuing small companies. The big question is: What kind of small company should you seek out? Small means different things. A tiny neighborhood laundromat, hardware store, or car dealership is an example of a small company. But a small company could also be a thriving cookie manufacturer selling products all over the United States. The latter company is the kind I'm talking about. It's what *Boston Globe* business writer John Case calls an "entrepreneurial, growth-oriented company." In his popular column "The Inc. Report," Case points out the average little company starts small and stays that way. The few jobs it creates are parceled out to a small number of employees or family members. But it's the entrepreneurial companies in all industries that generate the majority of new jobs. They grow aggressively, creating jobs along the way. Look around and you'll see hundreds of examples of companies that were once tiny, but feisty, upstarts. Apple Computer, Microsoft, Ben & Jerry's, Staples, and Little Caesar's are just a few classic examples.

The U.S. Small Business Administration (SBA) was thinking of the growth-oriented entrepreneurial enterprise when it defined a small company. According to the SBA, a small company has fewer than 500 employees or sales under $10 million; by contrast, midsize companies have sales under $100 million. There are about 20.5 million small businesses in the United States, generating two-thirds of all new jobs. Cognetics, Inc., an economics research firm based in Cambridge, MA, says companies with fewer than 100 employees created nearly all job growth from 1988 through the present.

Now you know why taking your chances with companies launched in incubators or enterprise zones could pay off handsomely. Many of these tiny start-ups will be tomorrow's industry leaders.

WHY SMALL COMPANIES OFFER BETTER CAREER PROSPECTS

Here are six reasons that small companies offer better career opportunities than large ones.

1. *No-nonsense, roll-up-your-sleeves attitude.* Many large and mid-size companies are weighed down in bureaucracy. You have to contend with politics, rules, and hierarchies in order to get things done. Not so in small companies. If something is deemed doable, the wheels start churning immediately.

2. *Greater willingness to take chances.* The best of the small companies are like toddlers learning to walk. They're so determined to stand on their feet unassisted, they keep at it until they succeed. They're also willing to take chances. In the process, they stumble, fall, and get right up and try all over again. It's that "I won't accept defeat" attitude that propels small companies to success.

3. *Rewards for innovation and creativity.* The best small companies are like hungry cheetahs after prey. They're sleek, fast, and graceful. They're lean operations determined to succeed. They're all about getting the best products or services to market in the most efficient way. One way to accomplish that end is by rewarding innovative and creative workers. Everything else takes a back seat.

4. *Rapid advancement.* Prized workers are rewarded quickly. Unlike large companies, small ones don't wait for yearly performance reviews or get enmeshed with the politics of seniority. If you're good, you'll reap benefits. Consistently boost the entrepreneur's bottom line and you'll bolt to the top.

5. *Profit participation.* Many smart entrepreneurs are willing to share their success, especially with major contributors. Beyond frequent promotions and raises, workers with money to invest ought to consider buying stock in the company or becoming small percentage partners. Why not snare a piece of the entrepreneur's dream? If the company meets all your criteria, from financial solvency to human chemistry, it's the best way to put a lock and key on the future.

6. *Quick hiring decisions.* I saved the best for last. Entrepreneurs running small companies don't have a nanosecond to waste. Unlike management in large companies, they're not about to spend months looking for new people. More likely than not, as soon as the right person appears, he or she is hired—often during the first interview. Typically, the process takes 2 to 3 weeks, sometimes less.

TAKE A FLYER ON A START-UP COMPANY

Start-ups are a crapshoot, yet ultimately offer the most exciting career opportunities. (Riskier yet are troubled companies, which we'll tackle in the next chapter.) The scary statistics are that most start-ups fail within their first 3 years, making them an exciting adventure. Unlike established companies, start-ups have to walk the treacherous gauntlet to profitability. They present the ultimate ground-floor opportunity. What better place to prove yourself? The overwhelmed entrepreneur is knee deep in aggravation, burdened with the hundreds of details of getting the company off the ground. He or she needs someone with your experience, confidence, and business smarts. Become indispensable during the live-or-die phase of the company and your future will be assured.

FAMILY-RUN COMPANIES OFFER MIXED OPPORTUNITIES

A healthy percentage of start-ups and established small companies are family-run operations. There is no middle ground here. They're either smooth, profitable, well-managed operations or rife with politics, intrigue, and infighting. Leon Danco, nationally known business consultant to family-run companies, reports that most family businesses die within 10 years because of discord within the ranks.

Warning: If the company's top jobs are held by family members, think twice about working there because you won't go very far. The majority of family-run companies are tiny mom-and-pop operations. Your best bet are the larger, more aggressive, multimillion-dollar entrepreneurial family-run organizations such as the thriving Quill Corporation in Lincolnshire, IL, that depend upon outside talent to keep the business afloat.

Before investigating career options, check out the company first. How long has it been in business? Most important, do only family members hold the best jobs?

CHECKING OUT SMALL COMPANIES

Researching small companies is easy. Plenty of current sources can tell you more than you need to know.

Print Sources

Beyond obvious print sources, which include daily papers and national business magazines such as *The Wall Street Journal, Forbes, Fortune, Nation's Business,* and *Entrepreneur,* take a look at the following.

Hoover's Reference Books. (The Reference Press, Inc., 6448 Highway 290 East, Suite E-104, Austin, TX 78723; 512-454-7778.) Company profiles in all the Hoover books contain operations overviews, company strategies, histories, key financial data for a 10-year period, product lists, executive names, headquarters addresses, and phone and fax numbers. All are updated annually.

Hoover's Masterlist of Major U.S. Companies 1993 contains data on 6200 companies and its *Computer Industry Almanac 1994* describes more than 2500 computer companies.

Hoover's Handbook of Emerging Companies contains one-page snapshots of well-known, high-profile leaders in their fields, plus smaller, lesser-known companies with explosive potential.

Dun & Bradstreet Inc. (Dun & Bradstreet Information Services Products, One Diamond Hill Road, Murray Hill, NJ 07974-0027; 800-526-0651.) The sprawling multimillion-dollar company that checks your credit ratings uses its database of over 10 million American companies to publish the following:

Dun's Regional Business Directory (three volumes) offers information on 20,000 public and private regional businesses.

Dun's Employment Opportunities Directory/The Career Guide explains hiring practices and employment opportunities at 5000 U.S. companies, providing corporate history, promising career options, education requirements, address, phone numbers, and contacts.

Most D&B products are available in well-stocked business libraries.

CorpTech (Woburn, MA; 800-333-8036.) The annual *CorpTech Directory* covers the entire high-tech arena, listing more than 35,000 U.S. public and private technology companies and rapidly growing firms with fewer than 100 employees. The company's Corporate Technology Information Services division publishes *The Technology Industry Growth Forecaster,* a four-page monthly newsletter, covering exciting private companies, new technologies, and promising locations.

On-Line Sources

Here are a few on-line sources offering timely business information.

NewsBank (New Canaan, CT; 800-762-8182.) The NewsBank database contains articles culled from 200 regional business publications serving 450 U.S. cities. It's a good source for tidbits about small privately held companies and divisions of bigger organizations not covered in large dailies.

Equifax National Decisions Systems (Encinitas, CA; 800-866-6510.) Equifax promotes a database of some 9.7 million businesses, a healthy percentage of which are companies with fewer than 10 employees. It is an excellent source for honing in on very specific information. *Example:* Tiny trucking companies in St. Johnsbury, VT, with fewer than 20 employees. The database provides basic information on location, sales, products, and contacts.

Predicasts Newsletter Database (Cleveland, OH; 800-321-6388.) Here's another offbeat source unknown to most job searchers. Journalists and company heads long ago discovered that newsletters are an incredible information source. The best of them offer timely, often exclusive, information. You may stumble on information gems found nowhere else.

Covering over 700 trade and business newsletters, Predicasts classifies them according to 48 industry codes, making it easy to find newsletters in your field. You may be pleasantly surprised when you uncover several valuable newsletters covering your industry. Professional newsletters can be expensive, however, with subscriptions running over $300 a year. Be creative and find ways to track them down. A colleague may get one; business libraries may carry others. I guarantee your trade organization also has the important ones neatly cataloged. It's worth the effort to hunt them down.

Now the lowdown on troubled companies, another potential job avenue that job searchers traditionally avoid.

CHAOS SPELLS OPPORTUNITY

Ailing companies need rescuers. You just might be the very person they're looking for—if you're up for the joust. It's human nature to avoid trouble. Who needs more problems? The very mention of a "troubled company" sends shivers up and down your spine. For good reason. Many of us were fired from companies that were on the brink of or in the throes of chaos. So why would any reasonably sane person seek out a sinking ship? What kind of lunatic or masochist would even suggest such madness? I confess, I would— but for good reason.

Chaos doesn't always mean personal disaster and hardship. It could also bring opportunity. Look beneath the flooding hull to see if the damage can be repaired and the boat righted.

James E. Challenger, president of international outplacement consulting firm Challenger, Gray & Christmas, advises veteran job searchers to pursue troubled companies. Contrary to what most job seekers believe, Challenger contends troubled companies that have made cuts or layoffs have a more urgent need for qualified people than do many economically fit companies.

Of the discharged managers Challenger counsels, some 40 percent get jobs at troubled companies. His advice: Disregard adverse news about a company—unless, of course, it is news of impending bankruptcy. Negative reports foster the illusion that no job possibilities exist at the company, when in fact the opposite is true. Bad news about layoffs is a signal of urgent opportunity. An alarm is blaring, cannons are firing. The company needs an infusion of talent—and pronto. You could be part of the new management regime.

HOW HEROES ARE BORN

In *When It Hits the Fan,* Gerald C. Meyers, former chairman of American Motors, insists that heroes are born in a crisis. Lee Iacocca's salvaging a troubled Chrysler is one of his favorite examples. The payoff for Iacocca was instant stardom, the ultimate career catapult. Of course, Iacocca is the exception, not the rule. How many businesspeople emerge as household names, their face as familiar as a movie star's?

But what's wrong with being a local hero? Save a failing company and you'll get more than a pat on the back and congratulations from well-wishers. You stand to get a powerful management position with a salary and perks to match. And what about hard-won respect? You're the godlike turnaround artist who helped bring a company back from the dead. Beyond securing yourself a powerhouse position, you've saved other people's jobs.

Imagine throwing caution to the wind and joining GM or IBM during 1993 when it was slashing jobs and restructuring its operations with a vengeance. GM's John F. Smith and IBM's new chairman and chief executive Louis V. Gerstner, Jr. were hell-bent on saving their companies. The world watched while these two men did their magic. Not ordinary companies by any stretch of the imagination, GM and IBM were the proud superstars of the 1950s, 1960s, and 1970s, the standard bearers of American industrialism. Together, the two companies employed more than 880,000 people in scores of cities and towns. IBM led the world in patent holdings and GM headed an industry that accounted for one in eight jobs in the United States. But like hundreds of others, the two multinational companies grew fat and unwieldy. Their commanding officers went about the nasty job of saving the company by dumping dead weight, buoying the losses with superstars who could do the work of five. Since 1986, IBM has shrunk its payroll from 406,000 to its present slim and trim 215,000.

Gerstner created cost-cutting task forces, dramatically improving efficiency and eliminating waste. An immediate result was speeding up the turnover of IBM's computer inventory. In 1993, the $10 billion inventory of computers turned over 2.8 times a year. In 1994, the inventory turned over 3.5 times, translating to about $2 billion in savings.

Beginning in 1991, GM's Smith aggressively cut costs by shrinking employment in North America by 74,000, or 23 percent. In

1991, the company lost $10.7 billion, before interest and taxes. Making a dramatic turnaround, in 1994, it made a $362 million profit. *Fortune* magazine praised the giant automaker, calling it "GM's $11 Billion Turnaround."

Imagine if you were one of the chosen recruits in either company. You gambled on its superstar managers turning the companies around. Your instincts proved right. Your reward? A starring position on the new management team.

But there is a flip side you ought to consider as well. Putting Walter Mitty fantasies aside, you could still go down with the ship. No matter how much effort you put out, sometimes nothing can be done to save a sinking company. If you think you lost out and made a poor decision, you're dead wrong. Either way, you win. Crisis presents opportunities available at no other time.

THREE ADVANTAGES OF CRISIS

Beyond making you a hero, crisis presents three other opportunities, according to Meyers.

1. *Chance to demonstrate talents.* If anyone secretly thought you were out of touch, dried up, and (I shudder to use the word) "old," here's a ready-made opportunity to prove you're a force to be reckoned with.

Taking advantage of a crisis can be likened to taking over for the ailing star of a successful Broadway play. If the understudy gives a brilliant performance, his or her career can be launched in one night. Sadly, many talented actors never have the opportunity to prove themselves. Getting a chance to be part of the team rescuing a sick company is not very different.

2. *High-priced skills.* A couple of decades ago, the term *crisis management* didn't exist. Today, prestigious business schools such as Carnegie Mellon and Wharton actually teach it. They're led by people like Meyers, who salvaged companies on the brink of disaster.

Thanks to rampant corporate turmoil, crisis management has become a high-priced specialty. Invest 6 months working for a troubled company and you've got a crash course in the new science. Better yet, you've captured marketable skills.

3. *Contacts and leads.*   Crisis is the ultimate networking experience. Do the best you can and you won't be forgotten. Virtually every contact—company brass, employees, vendors, clients, and customers—is a potential networking lead. Keep notes, get phone numbers, and most important stay in touch.

JUNGLE TACTICS FOR THE HEARTY

Those are the compelling advantages of working for a troubled company. No matter how potentially rewarding, however, it's not for everyone. Many of us don't have the temperament and nerves to endure nonstop stress. It's nothing to be ashamed of, either. If you don't have the constitution, don't even consider it. Here's what you can expect.

1. *Daily uncertainty.*   Every day is different. Gone is the comforting security of daily routines. During periods of crisis, new rules apply. It's a time of intense experimentation, with management trying everything possible to get the company on a profitable track. If you aren't flexible, you won't cut it.

2. *Long hours.*   The old 9-to-5 regimen goes right out the window. If you plan on giving this experience your best performance, expect to put in 10- and 12-hour days, maybe more. You might be working weekends too. Until the situation is resolved, or the company is buried, your job becomes your life. That fact had better be a turn-on, rather than a turnoff.

3. *Mounting responsibility.*   The more involved you become in the process of saving a sinking ship, the more you'll be doing. Chances are there's been a series of layoffs, making you part of a skeleton crew. That means you're doing the work of two, maybe three people. What's more, your responsibilities could change daily. One day you're directing sales and marketing efforts; the next you're supervising the loading dock or purchasing operations. You're a jack-of-all-trades, the consummate master of everything you touch.

4. *Numbing deadlines and short tempers.*   With creditors, bankers, and angry customers breathing down your neck, there's a good chance you're fighting the clock so that doors aren't padlocked for good. Your job is to help get the company back on track, producing exceptional products or services. That's a tall order when morale is poor and remaining staffers are waiting for the right moment to jump ship. Not everyone can take the kind of chances you can afford to take.

Expect new stress factors every day. A company warding off creditors is in a battle zone. Keeping your cool isn't easy. There will be days when nothing goes right and you rue the decision to get involved. But there'll also be days when everything goes right and you're experiencing incredible adrenaline highs.

Still interested? If you are, give it a try. One thing is certain: You won't be bored. Who's to say you won't walk in one day and discover your office furniture was repossessed or the doors padlocked by the sheriff's office? No joke. It's happening every day throughout corporate America.

Can you endure this kind of angst 7 days a week? If you're uncertain, find safer ground offering a more secure future.

FINDING TROUBLED COMPANIES

These days, finding troubled companies is easy. The signposts of trouble are all around. You'll find plenty just by reading the daily papers, watching the news, and staying plugged into your industry.

Warning signs: Planned layoffs, cashflow problems, sliding profits, product failures, facility closings, and rapid declines in stock prices, to name a few.

Making contact isn't difficult either. The fastest way is through a connection. The next-best strategy is a letter to the president or a major decision maker. Get right to the point. Sell the skills you think the company needs to overcome the crisis. Follow up in 5 days if people don't get back to you first. If you're lucky, you'll be called immediately. The response: "It takes guts to take a chance on an ailing company. When can we meet?"

Now, let's move on to safer ground and explore the nonprofit world.

NONPROFITS RESPECT TALENT AND EXPERIENCE

If you spent most of your career working for profit-making organizations (PMOs), it's hard getting a grasp on the nonprofit organizations (NPOs). Also called voluntary or private-sector industries, they represent yet another exciting job source you probably never considered.

To better understand how nonprofits fit into the total scheme of things, consider that the working world is carved into three parts: PMOs (comprising 80 percent of the population), government organizations (10 percent), and NPOs (10 percent). PMOs generate wealth; government, power; and NPOs, morality, mission, and public good. In PMOs, individuals or stockholders benefit directly from company activities. In NPOs, something is being done for the public good. In PMOs, start-up money often comes from investors seeking equity and a return on their investment; in NPOs, seed funding comes from government sources, foundations, corporate grants, or individual contributions.

IT'S NOT ABOUT MONEY: AN INSIDE LOOK AT NPOs

NPOs are a world unto themselves, with their own philosophy, language, and way of doing things. For true believers, working for a nonprofit is not just a job or career; it's a passion, a mission. They're making a statement. They're all about improving the quality of life (cleaning up the environment), ending disease (finding a cure for AIDS), advocating a cause (ending apartheid, wiping out illiteracy), and more.

Success for PMOs is measured in dollars; for NPOs, it's accomplishing a goal or achieving a purpose. No wonder the two don't understand each other. The key to success in an NPO is total dedication to an ideal. That's a far cry from devoting practically all your waking hours to making affordable widgets—and a pile of dough.

Fast Facts About Nonprofits

There are plenty of nonprofits from which to choose. Consider these compelling facts culled from the Independent Sector, a research organization based in Washington, DC:

- More than 1 million nonprofit organizations operate in the United States. Between 1977 and the present, nonprofits' share of total employment increased from 8.5 percent (8.8 million) to 10.4 percent (14.4 million).
- NPOs depend more on highly educated workers than do PMOs.
- More than half of total full- and part-time employment in NPOs is in the professional and executive/managerial occupational groups.
- Nearly 90 percent of all full-time jobs in NPOs fall under five broad occupational groups: professional specialty, administrative support, managerial and administrative, service, and technical and related support.

Where the Jobs Are

Below are the top nonprofit organizations, ranked by number of people employed:

1. Health services
   - Nursing
   - Hospitals and personal-care facilities
   - Outpatient-care and allied services
2. Educational/research
   - Private elementary and secondary schools
   - Private colleges and universities
   - Other (libraries, correspondence schools, and educational services)
   - Noncommercial educational, scientific, and research organizations

3. Religious organizations

4. Social and legal services
   - Individual and family services
   - Job training and related services
   - Child day-care services
   - Residential-care services

5. Civic, social, and fraternal organizations

6. Arts and culture
   - Radio and TV broadcasting
   - Producers and entertainers
   - Orchestras
   - Museums
   - Botanical and zoological gardens

7. Foundations

EMPLOYMENT TRENDS IN THE NONPROFIT WORLD

As with PMOs, trendy NPOs are tied to politically correct causes. They snare headlines, but more important, capture sizable funding. A few years ago, the environment was everyone's favorite cause; today, it's been beaten out by a number of health-care issues. At the top of the list is AIDS. Sadly, AIDS had to reach epidemic proportions before major dollars were funneled into NPOs caring for AIDS patients—and, more important, into research for a cure. As with any popular cause, it took fanfare, public outcry, and support among high-profile public figures—from politicians to household-name celebrities.

Who's to say what tomorrow's cause will be—the homeless, improving the plight of third-world countries, crime in the streets, the elderly? It really doesn't matter. Unlike the ephemeral fads of the profit-making world, the good work of NPOs endures. The world is improved because of them.

NPOs Don't Give a Hoot How Old You Are

The great news is NPOs aren't hung up about age, unlike PMOs. According to the Independent Sector, employees between the ages of 55 and 64 make up approximately 11 percent of NPOs, compared with 8 percent of PMOs. The reason is that NPOs are gobbling up thousands of downsized professionals. And many intuitive PMO managers who see the writing on the wall are jumping ship and moving to NPOs. It's a win-win situation all around. Fiftyish workers are taking jobs in organizations delighted to get seasoned pros.

No Stigma Against Job Hopping

Whereas job hopping has only recently gained respectability among PMOs, NPOs never frowned upon it. In fact, NPOs regard job hopping as an excellent tactic for getting experience. The more organizations for which you've worked, the more you bring to the table. The ideal candidate is someone who's worked for both large and small organizations. Well rounded, he or she can function in any kind of organization.

Rapid Advancement...Lower Salaries

The bad news is nonprofits don't pay as well as PMOs. Among professional specialties, salaries range about 10 to 25 percent below those of PMOs. And despite dramatic growth, most NPOs are underfunded and understaffed. They're constantly slashing budgets and forced to function under tight budgetary restraints. They're masters at scrimping.

The good news is that pay is inching up and there is a constant need for flexible, hardworking people willing to pitch in. Skills honed in the profit-making world can be easily transferred to the nonprofit sector. Rather than consider it a career change, think of it as a new direction.

Equally compelling, you can move up quickly. NPOs are always looking for talented people. Yet the traits they're looking for are not very different from those demanded by PMOs. Uppermost, NPOs depend upon smart, articulate, grounded idealists bursting with energy who can get things done. The more commanding your presence, the better your chances of going to the top.

Among the top jobs, NPOs are desperate for fund raisers. These are the folks who bring in the bucks, keeping the organization running and the salaries paid. If you were a top salesperson in your last job, odds are excellent you'd make a dynamite fund raiser—provided you're totally committed to the NPO's cause. Some high-ranking

NPO executives would balk at this analogy; nevertheless, top-notch fund raisers are masterful salespeople.

Raising money is an art. It's sophisticated selling of the first order. Rather than pushing a product or service, you're selling a cause or ideal. Getting people to buy in and reach for their checkbook to support that cause is a challenging and gratifying job. Designing the materials and strategies to accomplish this end takes creativity and insight. Whereas selling is the fast-track skill leading to a corner office in a PMO, fund raising can be the steppingstone to the top NPO slot—executive director.

STRATEGIES FOR LANDING A JOB

Two strategies are recommended for landing a job with an NPO. The first and obvious tactic is to simply apply, the same way you'd approach a PMO. If you have contacts or, better yet, know an insider who can recommend you, you've lucked out. This is the fastest way to get your foot in the door. However, not everyone is so fortunate.

Many NPOs have a reputation for being quirky, open-minded, and ultraliberal. But the sobering truth is most hire people the same way as PMOs do. They insist upon experience. It's the Catch-22 charade all over again. How do you get experience if no one will give you a job? Before you sprint toward the nearest open window, the answer is: It's a lot easier getting experience in an NPO than it is in a PMO.

The second job-getting strategy is to volunteer to help out. It's that simple. NPOs depend on volunteers. Many are desperate for them. According to the Independent Sector, approximately 98 million Americans volunteer an average of 4 hours per week, totaling 20.5 billion hours a year. The estimated value of this volunteer time is well over $170 billion. Practically every major nonprofit agency from the American Cancer Society to the Boys and Girls Club of America utilizes a small army of volunteers who pitch in and help.

Another plus is that volunteerism has jumped dramatically. New York City's Voluntary Action Center, for instance, reported that volunteering rose 30 percent between 1994 and 1995. Many authorities attribute the sudden interest in volunteering to rampant downsizing and the recession. I lean more toward the former reason.

Corporate refugees can find new skills, purpose, or just something to do. Keep in mind that every volunteer is not after a job. Deeply committed people see volunteering as a social duty. Some professionals deem it an impressive notch on their résumés, as well as an elegant networking avenue. Still others use it to kill time because they have nothing better to do.

VOLUNTEERING IS A RESPECTED JOB-CONQUERING TACTIC

Unfortunately, NPOs don't keep track of the number of volunteers they hire for paying jobs. I've heard countless stories of a volunteer winding up with a paying job through sheer accident. The more turned on they were by the work, the more committed they became. Five or six hours of volunteer time escalated to 10, 15, and 20 hours. Within a year's time, the volunteer was in a full-time salaried position.

NPOs like to promote from within. If a position opens up and you happen to be a well-liked, self-motivated workaholic warrior, you stand an excellent chance of being offered a job. There are no guarantees, but the odds are excellent.

There are other pluses to volunteering. Uppermost, it's a great way to find out how an NPO works. If you're willing to roll up your sleeves and pitch in, you can sample a smorgasbord of jobs—from addressing envelopes to cold-call fund raising to writing grants. Think of volunteering as an apprenticeship. Many nonprofits work volunteers harder than staffers. Understaffed nonprofits will jump at the chance to exploit your talents.

Before you even consider a paying job with an NPO, find out if you enjoy working there. Check out the people, bureaucracy, politics, and culture. Like PMOs, each nonprofit has its own culture. As a rule, small underfunded NPOs tend to be more aggressive, open-minded, and less bureaucratic than sprawling international ones. If you're a hyperkinetic dynamo, you can bolt through the ranks quickly. The best way to earn star status is by writing a brilliant grant that captures a few million dollars.

You may find that you love the cause, but are not impressed with the organization. Next move: Check out another NPO promoting the same cause.

Lastly, whether you move on or stay on to land a paying job, volunteering plugs you into a vast network of leads and contacts.

A UNIVERSE OF OPPORTUNITIES TO CHOOSE FROM

Finding the NPO that matches the cause you're passionate about isn't difficult. There are no shortage of NPOs and you don't have to look far to find them.

The choices range from giants like the YMCA or YWCA, March of Dimes, CARE, and American Lung Association to prestigious advocacy groups such as the Sierra Club, the Nature Conservancy, and the National Audubon Society. There are also headline-grabbing feisty organizations like the well-publicized Amnesty International of the USA, the worldwide organization protecting human rights, as well as hundreds of grassroots projects. If you enjoy working with teenagers, there's the Boys and Girls Club of America. About 1450 local chapters operate throughout the United States, serving 1.83 million youngsters, ages 6 to 18. If drug prevention is a pet cause, look to Phoenix House, Daytop Village, or a similar organization.

That's for starters. Once you do some homework, you'll discover it's easier than you think to match cause and NPO. Consider the following:

Animal rights   American Society for the Prevention of Cruelty to Animals

Antisemitism   Anti-Defamation League of B'Nai B'Rith

Control of nuclear testing   Greenpeace USA, Inc.

Age discrimination   Gray Panthers Project Fund

Control of firearms   Handgun Control, Inc.

Free enterprise and limited government   The Heritage Foundation

You get the idea. Practically every cause has an NPO serving it. There are even national services that will do your homework for you and match you to a suitable NPO. Two such respected organizations are the Volunteers of America (800-462-1715) and the Points of

Light Foundation in Washington, DC (800-879-5400). One of the largest human services agencies, Volunteers of America (founded in 1896) offers a raft of programs for children, families, the elderly, criminals, alcohol and drug abusers, and people with mental and physical disabilities.

Points of Light was created during the Bush administration to tackle social problems. Its network of volunteer centers throughout the United States helps communities mobilize people for charitable service.

Additionally, most large cities have volunteer referral centers, which are actually clearinghouses that match people to nonprofit organizations.

FINDING NPOs

For information about NPOs, check out these sources.

Organizations

The Society for Nonprofit Organizations (6314 Odana Road, #1, Madison, WI 53719; 800-424-7367). Provides basic information about nonprofit organizations. Publishes *Nonprofit World* magazine six times per year.

The Independent Sector (1828 L Street, NW, Suite 1200, Washington, D.C. 20036; 202-223-8100). This national organization tracks the nonprofit industry. Its yearly *Nonprofit Almanac* is full of vital statistics and information covering the entire nonprofit sector.

National Charities Information Bureau (19 Union Square West, 6th Floor, New York, NY 10003; 212-929-6300). Founded in 1918, the bureau is well respected as the NPO watchdog, monitoring 250 NPOs that solicit donations from the public. Call for a quick reading on an NPO's finances and management.

Periodicals

The Chronicle of Philanthropy is a biweekly newspaper monitoring the world of charitable giving. Subscriptions, 800-347-6969; office (202) 466-1200.

The Non-Profit Times is a monthly magazine for nonprofit executives. (201) 734-1700.

ACCESS: Networking in the Public Interest, is a New York-based clearinghouse for nonprofit jobs throughout the United States. It publishes *Community Jobs: The National Employment Newspaper for the Non-Profit Sector* and regional twice-monthly editions of the newsletter *Community Jobs,* serving New York and Washington, D.C. (212) 475-1001.

Books

Jossey-Bass (350 Sansome St., San Francisco, CA 94104-1310) publishes a number of excellent books on nonprofits and government. Here are a few worth looking at: *Government and the Third Sector,* edited by Gidron, Kramer, and Salamon; *Nonprofit Almanac,* a vital reference tool for anyone involved with nonprofit organizations; *The Makings of a Philanthropic Fund-raiser,* by Ronald Alan Knott; *Strategic Planning for Fund-raising,* by Wesley E. Lindahl; *The Commons,* by Roger A. Lohmann; and two independent-sector publications, *The Nonprofit Sector in the Global Community* and *Governing, Leading, and Managing Nonprofit Organizations.*

A Guide for Giving: 250 Charities and How They Use Your Money, by Howard Gershen (Pantheon Books). This excellent source gives a bird's-eye view of a wide range of charities across the United States. It lists each organization's address, telephone number, purpose, size, income, and financial data.

Finding a Job in the Nonprofit Sector, edited by William Wade (12300 Twinbrook Parkway, Suite 450, Rockville, MD 20852). Ranks 5000 of the largest nonprofit organizations by name, address, phone number, description, and estimated annual income. About 1000 listings offer contact name, total number of employees, types of jobs, benefits, and tips on contacting the organization.

Finally, check the yellow, white, and blue pages of your telephone directory. Under the heading "Volunteer," you'll find a variety of federal, state, and city agencies.

NONPROFITS AREN'T PERFECT

A last word. No matter how noble the cause, NPOs, like PMOs, aren't perfect. They're run by fallible humans. Start out separating the organization from its cause and you won't be disillusioned. Whether it's a tiny save-the-world NPO run by former hippies who think Woodstock was cosmic or a sprawling mega-agency headed by straight-laced, clean-shaven former government bureaucrats, expect in-fighting, foot-dragging, and backstabbing. Politics are part of the organizational game.

Now on to opportunities in the exploding temporary service industry.

TEMP YOUR WAY INTO A JOB

Remember when temping meant performing low-level office or manual jobs about which you never spoke? When you couldn't find a job and could barely scrape up money to cover next month's rent, temping saved the day. Anything to bring in some cash. Temping meant working as a bookkeeper, secretary, stenographer, or maintenance worker. In the old days, temping was grunt or back-office work. It was tide-you-over, bread-and-butter work until you found a *real* job to boast about. It was, in short, very temporary—hopefully, 2 to 3 months at the most.

It's a whole other game these days. Temping has gained respectability. What's more, temp work doesn't actually have to be temporary. A temp position can last 3 weeks to 3 years. In this crazy job market, a temporary job can be more secure than many full-time positions.

Thousands of frustrated workers dumped by large companies because of across-the-board cuts have turned their backs on the paycheck culture and opted for a life of temping. They enjoy the lifestyle because they can stop and start work whenever they please. If you thrive on adventure, relish the excitement of testing new jobs, and enjoy meeting new people, temping can be a lot of fun. And if you're experienced in a high-demand occupation—accountant, computer programmer, medical technician, nurse—you'll find plenty of options throughout the United States. Depending on your field and skill level, the pay can be excellent. Most of the large, established firms pay competitive (or better) salaries.

The best part is, temp firms are looking for candidates with *your* qualifications. That spells opportunities for workers 50 and over. Hundreds of temp firms across the country are begging for qualified people to fill temporary full- and part-time positions. Some economists project that in 10 to 15 years, the nation could be in a major bind trying to find qualified employees. Employers are finally wising up to the fact that older workers fit the bill. So don't doubt your marketability for a second.

Stay with me. I'm going to tell you how the sprawling temp world works and point you toward some mouthwatering opportunities. First, let's clear up any misconceptions by examining what a temp firm is and how it works.

DON'T CONFUSE TEMP FIRMS WITH EMPLOYMENT AGENCIES

Don't be embarrassed if you're not quite sure about the operations of a temp firm. Most people make the mistake of confusing them with employment agencies. When you understand the difference, you'll see why temp firm owners practically levitate when their organizations are called employment agencies. They insist upon being called temporary help companies or temporary service firms.

Employment agencies act as a third party, pairing workers with companies. Their fee is a percentage of the applicant's first-year salary. Once an applicant is placed at a company, the relationship with the employment agency ends. Not so with temp firms. Although you work at an assigned location, your employer actually is the temp firm, which is paid a commission or a markup on your hourly salary.

Pay? A temp firm marks up hourly pay between 20 and 35 percent, depending upon your skill level. An accountant, computer programmer, or paralegal earns a lot more than a secretary or stenographer, for example. Some temps even earn between $20 and $35 an hour.

A VARIETY OF JOBS PLUS BENEFITS

To show you how far temp firms have come, many of the established players provide their workers with health insurance at discounted rates, vacation pay, profit sharing, and referral bonuses. For example, Adia Personnel Services, a 600-office firm, gives its workers $200 vacation pay after temping 1500 hours and $400 after 2000 hours. Even smaller temp firms offer enticing perks. Advantage, Inc., based in Greenwich, CT, recently started a profit-sharing plan for its 8000 employees. Workers are vested after completing 1000 hours.

Here are the basic skills that temp firms supply to clients.

- *Office/clerical*—secretaries, general office clerks, receptionists, typists, and word processing operators
- *Technical*—computer programmers, computer systems analysts, designers, drafters, editors, engineers, and illustrators
- *Professional*—occupations in accounting (accountants, auditors), law (paralegals and attorneys), sales, and marketing, as well as those in management (middle and senior levels)
- *Medical*—registered and practical nurses and technicians for hospitals, nursing homes, outpatient clinics, and home health care

As the temp industry grows, more firms are serving particular industries or professions. Some temp firms specialize in financial services or health care, for example. Other firms are developing specialties in graphic arts, accounting, marketing/advertising, or sales positions.

I've saved the best for last. Here's some news guaranteed to whet your appetite. Temp agencies even specialize in placing execs. That could mean a job out there with your name on it. *Executive Recruiter News* (*ERN*), a newsletter covering the executive search industry, identified over 200 multimillion-dollar firms placing *flex-execs*, otherwise known as executive temporaries or interim managers. *ERN* publisher Jim Kennedy has a wealth of observations about the executive temporary market. Here is a summary:

- More firms are offering temp exec placement services.
- More executives at all levels are pursuing temp work.
- More companies, downsized to the limit, need interim execs for caretaker management (to cover open positions), restructuring, and mentoring, and—perhaps the biggest area—for special projects.
- Professional-level temps will earn more than $1 billion this year and placement firms will generate about $100 million in fees placing them.
- Since 1990, the number of firms serving this market has grown from 40 to 205.

- Most firms entering temp exec placement in the past 4 years have stayed with this area and most experts see it as a long-term growth trend.

Take the hint and pick up a copy of Kennedy's *Directory of Executive Temporary Placement Firms*. For information, contact Kennedy Publications, Templeton Road, Fitzwilliam, NH 03447 (603-585-6544).

MAJOR PLAYERS ARE DOING GANGBUSTER BUSINESS

If you harbor doubts about whether the temp industry means megabucks, ponder this fact: The industry is—are you ready?—a $25 billion business. Since 1992, the Staffing Industry Stock Index, which measures the collective share price performance of eight publicly traded staffing companies, has been gaining ground steadily on the S&P 500 Stock Index.

The U.S. Bureau of Labor Statistics reports that 1 in every 109 jobs is classified a temp position. That translates to more than 1 million temp jobs in the United States, compared with 184,391 in 1970.

The temp work force is growing 10 times as fast as the permanent labor pool for a number of reasons. At the head of the list stands rampant and continuous downsizing as the most significant cause of the dramatic surge in the temp market. Forget everything you were told about job hunting. Bottom-line thinking rules corporate boardrooms. Why make a long-term hiring commitment if you don't have to? More and more companies are hiring workers the same way they purchase inventory—on a just-in-time basis. It means they pay for precisely what they need when they need it, without being burdened with benefits, pension or profit-sharing plans, and medical coverage. Temp firms are meeting this demand and they're doing a hell of a job. When you think about it, it's not a bad arrangement. Companies instantly find great people and workers are well paid for their talents.

If you're curious about who the industry superstars are, take a look at the 36 top temp firms in the United States. They're ranked by net income, starting with the biggest producer.

The 36 Top Temp Firms in the United States

1. Manpower, Inc.
2. Olsten Corporation
3. Kelly Services Inc.
4. Adia Personnel Services Inc.
5. Robert Half International Inc.
6. CDI Corp.
7. Keane Inc.
8. Interim Services Inc.
9. Norell Corp.
10. Watsco Inc.
11. Computer Horizons Corp.
12. Right Management Consultants Inc.
13. Brandon Systems Corporation
14. Alternative Resources Group
15. Computer Task Group Inc.
16. On Assignment Inc.
17. Staff Builders Inc.
18. Careerstaff Unlimited Inc.
19. Uniforce Temporary Personnel Inc.
20. Barrett Business Services Inc.
21. National TechTeam Inc.
22. Butler International Inc.
23. Hooper Holmes Inc.
24. RCM Technologies Inc.
25. C.H. Heist Corp.
26. Personnel Management Inc.
27. Labor Ready Inc.
28. Winston Resources Inc.
29. General Employment Enterprises Inc.
30. Star Multi Care Services
31. Digital Solutions Inc.
32. Joule Inc.
33. GTS Duratek Inc.
34. Employee Solutions Inc.
35. Of Counsel Enterprises Inc.
36. Hospital Staffing Inc.

JUST WHAT THE DOCTOR ORDERED

I can read your mind. You're thinking, "Why waste my time temping when I want a permanent job?" Here's why.

Working at a temp job can be an incredible morale booster. Even if you don't need the money, you'll reap psychological rewards taking a lower-level temp job until something more substantial surfaces. You're out in the working world every day. When you think about it, that's worth more than dollars.

Since temp jobs are generally easier to find than permanent ones (especially if you have the skills that employers are looking for), temping can be an immediate catapult back into the job market. Why wait around the house waiting for the phone to ring when there's an opportunity to jump back into the fray?

Temping is a made-to-order networking platform. Beyond constantly meeting new people, temping offers an opportunity to shop the marketplace for the right job. Similarly, many companies use it as a platform to audition people for permanent jobs. Although you shouldn't bank on a job offer, countless employers have asked temps to stay on, often in better positions than the ones for which they were initially hired.

Like nonprofit organizations, temp firms have no bias against job hopping. The more experience you have in a variety of businesses, the more marketable you are. Most temp firms encourage their workers to register with several temp companies. They deem it an opportunity to earn, learn, and stay marketable. Everyone profits.

NAME YOUR HOURS

Most temp firms concentrate on filling full-time temporary positions. However, depending on business conditions, they also get their fair share of part-time jobs. You're more likely to find these positions at big temp firms, such as Olsten Temporary Services and Manpower International Inc., two of the country's largest.

Manpower is testing a 24-hour service that specializes in part-time and weekend workers. Serving a large metropolis like New York City, which never shuts down, Manpower has observed a marked demand for late-afternoon (second shift), late-night (third or lobster shift) and weekend workers. Law, accounting, advertising, and financial services firms, for example, constantly need people for brief, rushed deadline assignments. If the 24-hour service proves successful in New York, Manpower expects to replicate it in other major cities.

Take the hint: If a major player like Manpower is exploring this part-time market, assume that other temp firms will be jumping in behind them. Nose around and see what you can find. It's an opportunity to hold down two temp jobs at the same time. One may be an off-hour or weekend assignment, another a part-time weekday job. Without killing yourself, you can play the field and get a better reading on the market.

Don't spin your wheels by randomly calling firms that advertise in the newspaper want ads. The fastest way to locate temp firms is by checking the Yellow Pages under "Employment Contractors." You'll find quarter- and half-page ads touting their specialties.

WATCH OUT FOR THE BAD GUYS—AND ASK QUESTIONS

Without a doubt, the temp industry has cleaned up its act. Most temp firms are reputable and ethical, but as with any industry, expect some bad apples in the bunch. They're easy to spot.

Be wary of high-pressure salespeople promising the world and delivering little. Like they say, if it sounds too good to be true, chances are it is. To attract and keep talented workers, some temp firms promise impressive short-term jobs in blue-chip firms, without giving details. They'll fail to tell you they concentrate on supplying low-level office help—jobs you'd consider only if you couldn't pay the rent. If you harbor doubts or suspicions, ask questions.

Ethical firms hide nothing. From the outset, everything is spelled out—job location, responsibilities, pay, and length of assignment. Like any employer, the temp firm will issue you a W-2 form, rather than a 1099 form for independent contractors or consultants. A W-2 means you're entitled to workers' compensation and unemployment insurance; a 1099 does not. If the temp firm says you'll be sent a 1099 and be paid in 3 to 4 weeks when the client pays its bill, head for the door. Not only is it a bogus temp firm, it's violating the Fair Labor Standards Act.

Use common sense and let your instincts guide you. The office setup alone tells you a lot about the operation. I'd have serious reservations if I walked into a makeshift, dingy office. Most successful temp firms are upscale, affluent operations emitting positive vibes. The reception area and office staff provide your first clues. If the waiting room looks like a bus station, the office furniture is made of cheap plastic, and the staff appears condescending, rude, or poorly dressed, make a speedy exit. Why contend with a sleazy outfit when there are plenty of reputable, professional firms delighted to have your business?

If the temp world doesn't get your juices going, consider creating your own job. The next chapter shows you how.

CREATE YOUR OWN JOB...EVEN YOUR OWN COMPANY

The job market, while tough, is also exciting. In Chap. One, I discussed how a vast global marketplace has created new opportunities. But that was only to whet your appetite. Now I'm going to tell you just how exciting—make that *thrilling*—this market really can be.

Fierce competition for market share and profits has upgraded our standards and broadened our perspective. More important, it's created a competitive marketplace in which just surviving—forget about racking up megaprofits—has been elevated to a 24-hour obsession.

Companies, tiny to multinational, are desperate to find great people. If you plan to throw impressive downsizing statistics in my face, forget it. I've seen them all. What's more, it's old news. Downsizing is a fact of life. And it's not going away. Expect more cutbacks, layoffs, and corporate ghost towns for the remainder of the 1990s and beyond. But that's not the issue. Get beyond the buzzword and understand its real meaning—downsizing is a sterile word for dumping unnecessary human baggage. Just because corporate America continues to shed calories doesn't mean it no longer needs talented people. In fact, it needs them more than ever. The difference is, businesses are not looking for traditional, run-of-the-mill workers who show up and merely do their jobs. Instead, they want talented superstars with the management skills, energy, intuition, and plain common sense necessary to pilot organizations into the millennium. They're hungry for candidates with competitive skills who can survive an erratic marketplace in which tomorrow's widgets are already on the assembly line.

The best part is employers are bending the rules and sidestepping traditional hiring standards to find these workers. What worked in the past won't work in the future. Employers once demanded blue-chip candidates with Ivy League diplomas and experience from *Fortune* 500 companies. These staff members were politically correct button-down corporate clones that companies like IBM once prided themselves on hiring. Look what happened to Big Blue and hundreds of others. It has taken a while, but employers are now discovering that fancy titles from big companies are only a shallow indicator of talent.

THE DEATH OF THE JOB

That's not the half of it. Maybe you don't realize it, but like thousands of others scorned by employers that promised lifetime jobs, you've been liberated. You never have to work the way you did in the past. The reason is that the conventional job has gone the way of the dinosaur. William Bridges, author of *JobShift*, has put the "job" on the list of endangered species. Many organizations are well on their way to being what Bridges calls "dejobbed." That's the hot new buzzword for getting work done without hiring full-timers for conventional jobs. It means hiring temps or contract/project workers and leasing employees.

Bridges explains that prior to the Industrial Revolution, there was no such thing as a job per se, in which someone reported to work and did the same tasks 8 hours a day, 5 days a week. Instead, people worked on a "shifting cluster of tasks in a variety of locations on a schedule set by the sun, the weather, and the needs of the day." Only when work started to be packaged in factories and companies began emerging in a newly industrialized nation at the turn of the nineteenth century did the job emerge.

At the time, the concept behind a job made sense. Yet Bridges asserts it was a flawed social artifact destined for a brief life. The present marketplace is living proof. Remember when a job not only meant doing the same thing every day, but also represented a source of financial and emotional security? Back in the old days when you worked for a Big Blue clone, healthy companies actually took care of their flock. In the best of circumstances, they were surrogate mommies and daddies. You reported to the same place and hung out with the same people year in and year out. Lifestyles were spun around your employer.

Any futurist will tell you it won't be long before nomadic workers are operating out of cars, in airports, on buses, and at shifting workplaces. All the office equipment needed to run a multimillion-dollar company will be crammed into an attaché case. The modern company, according to Bridges, is rapidly being transformed from a structure built out of jobs into a field of "work needing to be done." This means work will no longer be departmentalized. Like the early craftspeople who fashioned their own work styles, modern workers must be creative chameleons—adaptable, flexible, multifaceted, veritable learning sponges capable of spinning on a dime and doing something completely different tomorrow.

It's already happening. Bridges' reading of the present and future job market is right on the money. The astute worker of the 1990s must forget about jobs completely and focus on "work needing to be done." Present an employer with the best (most efficient and profitable) way to achieve a goal and you're on the payroll. In essence, you're creating your own job by making yourself indispensable. Make sense? You bet it does. And you've got the background and skills to do it. Just activate your gray matter and you'll find a way.

"TELL ME WHAT TO DO!"

Put it all together and you'll discover a compelling new business environment in which to create your own job. Smart entrepreneurs are wising up and listening to experienced pros like you, people who can spot and solve problems. That spells *job creation*, particularly in this elastic market.

The career gurus never told you not to apply for jobs the way you did in the past. You've got insight and abilities that your younger counterparts don't. These are the priceless skills allowing you to spot opportunities no one else sees. That's what creating your own job is all about.

Start the process by making the assumption that employers don't always know what they want. Job descriptions are the best example. Countless professionals have told me their actual jobs are far different from the capsulized job descriptions which brought them to the company. This is especially true in small companies. Only weeks after being hired, employees found themselves doing countless chores that weren't even hinted at in their job descriptions.

It's easy to understand why this happens. Most entrepreneurs are guilty of minimizing a job. It's usually because they previously handled the job by rote. When translated to paper, it's inadequately explained. If it takes the entrepreneur 2 days to complete an essential part of a task, assume it'll take anyone else twice as long.

Employers lack objectivity because they live and breathe their business 7 days a week. No wonder they don't always know what a job entails or the talents and skills needed to run their organization. Countless entrepreneurs find themselves at a dangerous impasse once their businesses reach a certain plateau. To move to the next level, entrepreneurs must bring in professional managers or perish. Often, it's an advisory board, an accountant or attorney, or maybe colleagues or friends who present the business owner with irrefutable logic. It usually sounds like this: "Your energy and vision have taken the company this far. But the company has gotten so big, there is no way you can run it by yourself. You need people with skills you don't have."

Naturally, the entrepreneur will balk, insisting it's a waste of money. No one understands the business better than its founder. But if our weary entrepreneur is reasonably mature and has a solid grip on reality, he or she will agree to hiring fresh blood.

This is where you enter the picture.

FINDING JOB-CREATING OPPORTUNITIES

Plenty of entrepreneurs who have reached that critical plateau could use your help. For some, it's the $5 or $10 million sales mark; for others, it's $20, $40, or $50 million. By the same token, many start-ups are desperately in need of seasoned managers to guide them into adolescence.

Surprisingly, finding these opportunities is easier than you think. It starts with a mindset, sort of like an antenna tuning into companies with job creation possibilities. What about your network? Heads of trade associations, for example, may point you toward opportunities. Don't forget the hidden market sources mentioned in Chap. Eleven. Companies launched in business incubators and enterprise zones are more likely to be open to creative suggestions than established companies.

MAKE THEM AN OFFER THEY CAN'T REFUSE

Now the plot thickens. Once you find a company with an obvious need, it's time to shift into second gear and make the connection. Remember, you're trail blazing. You're doing something that's never occurred to most job searchers. There are no rules or precedents. You're creating them as you go along. The best way to make contact is by writing a letter, not unlike the one you're going to be preparing in the next chapter, when you toss out your résumé. The difference is that here you'll spend most of your time pointing up a critical need and showing how your qualifications can meet it.

Consider the sample letter on the following page.

Note that our clever job searcher had the good sense not to ask for a job. He also didn't make the hard sell by reeling off a lengthy list of prior jobs and titles. He merely whet the reader's appetite, driving home the point that he was a seasoned professional who knew the food industry. He's shooting for an appointment so he can sell himself face to face. The letter's intent is to pique the reader's curiosity: "This man knows the cookie industry. He makes sense. Maybe I ought to see him. What do I have to lose?"

The idea is to get yourself in the door and make a dynamite impression. Asking for a job straight out is the worst thing you can do. You'll put off the entrepreneur. Her first thought, "The last thing I need is another cash drain."

When you meet this skeptical entrepreneur, consider asking to work on a project as a consultant to prove your worth. Show your value and your negotiating position jumps a hundredfold. More on selling yourself brilliantly in Chap. Nineteen.

"I COULD RUN THIS COMPANY MYSELF"

Creating your own job could point you to still more exciting vistas, such as launching your own company. In a word: entrepreneurialism. Creating a job is risky enough; building a company is even scarier, because the odds are stacked against you from the onset. The U.S. Small Business Administration reports that approximately

24 Huntington Lane
Mansfield, Ohio XXXXX
January 1, 19XX

Dear Ms. Smollett:

I've taken the liberty of writing to tell you how I can help you better accomplish your goal of making Tempte Cookies the premier low calorie/fat-free line in the United States.

I've spent the better part of my career working in strategic planning for national cookie/cracker companies such as Keebler, Nabisco, and Quaker Oats and, more recently, as a senior marketing executive. Over my 25-year career, I've watched the industry change from hundreds of small independent companies to its present state, in which a half-dozen large multinationals dominate the market.

Don't get me wrong. I'm not telling you how to run your company, but rather am pointing out market strategies and niches you might not have considered. In this fiercely competitive marketplace, it takes more than great products to capture fickle consumers. If you'd give me 30 minutes of your time, I'd like to outline a marketing strategy that can better position your products, separating them from your competitors'.

Over the next week, I will call to arrange a mutually convenient time. I look forward to meeting with you.

Sincerely,

Thomas Hardy, Jr.

three out of five companies perish within their first 3 years of operation. But that hasn't stopped anyone from trying. Thanks to corporate downsizing, record numbers of gutsy folks test the entrepreneurial waters each year. According to Paul D. Reynolds, Coleman Foundation professor of entrepreneurial studies at Marquette University in Milwaukee, more people are starting companies in any given year than are getting married. Reynolds says—are you ready?—roughly 1 in every 25 adult Americans is trying to get a business off the ground. He figures the number of these prospective company owners (approximately 7 million) exceeds the entire population of Massachusetts or Missouri.

The above numbers are awesome. Thousands of corporate refugees feel entrepreneurship is their salvation. They're quickly finding there's a lot more to it than fantasies of freedom, wealth, and power. The fact is, few successful entrepreneurs actually enjoy such perks because they compulsively work, afraid they'll lose it all if they ease up on the reins for a second.

Be objective and think practically. That's easier said than done when you are soothing a bruised ego after being dumped by a company that swore lifetime allegiance. No wonder entrepreneurship seems attractive. The simple truth is not everyone is cut out to be an entrepreneur—it's no crime if you don't fit the profile.

THE FRENETIC LIFE OF A BUSINESS OWNER

Entrepreneurship means the proverbial buck stops with you. Success or failure rests solely in your mortal hands. Entrepreneurship also equates to working long, hard, endless hours, making tough decisions by yourself, bucking the tides, and standing by your beliefs when everyone around you insists you should be carted away. Unless you luck out and your business takes off immediately, count on doing big-time suffering.

Does the above seem absolutely repulsive? If you think prison time sounds more attractive, I've spared you the hardship, aggravation, and maybe the cost of a shrink. But what sounds like masochism to most people is actually a turn-on to entrepreneurs. This is the reason that entrepreneurs are an odd breed. Where most of us see problems and uncertainty, entrepreneurs envision opportunity. *Boston Globe* columnist John Case hit the nail on the head when he said entrepreneurs are blessed (or cursed) with the ability to spot business opportunities *anywhere*. He calls them the Manhattan cabbies of the business world. Says Case, "Pedal to the metal, they dart through openings the rest of us don't notice until it's too late."

Now that you've gotten a capsulized picture of the entrepreneurial lifestyle, here's a quick test to see if you can cut it. Can you live without the following?

- The prestige of a corporate position
- Easy access to the resources of a corporation
- The supportive feedback of coworkers
- Regular paychecks
- Paid holidays, sick leave, and vacations
- Paid medical and retirement packages

In sum, can you live without routines and with megadoses of uncertainty? Still interested in being an entrepreneur?

CAN ENTREPRENEURSHIP BE TAUGHT?

Some experts question my sanity, but I'm convinced an entrepreneurial gene exists that provides business creators with the foundation—talent, drive, and vision—for entrepreneurial success. If such a gene is ever discovered, academics could stop arguing over whether entrepreneurship can be taught. Some 300 colleges and universities across the United States insist it can. To prove it, they offer a battery of courses and degree programs in the business creation process.

But many skeptics, like myself, insist entrepreneurship really can't be taught. Professor William D. Bygrave at Boston's Babson College says you can teach entrepreneurial fundamentals, strategies, and tools of the trade. But if the natural talent is missing, you don't have a prayer.

In other words, you can study entrepreneurial skills until the cows come home, but if you don't have what experts have identified as the "entrepreneurial personality," your chances of succeeding are slim.

The entrepreneurial personality is made up of traits shared by all entrepreneurs. They include refreshingly unscientific terms like "streetfighter personality," "self-starter," "highly motivated," "workaholic/compulsive personalities," "creative-problem solver," and "ability to turn adversity into a learning experience." True entrepreneurs have the tenacity and persistence of pit bulls. Their capacity to endure stress, pain, and hardship seems almost inhuman. They figure it's the price you pay for building something of your own. They may be right. If you think holding down a job is tough, imagine the angst of getting a company off the ground, cementing deals, and making promises to vendors when there's no guarantee *you'll* be in business next month. Although they'll seldom admit it, smart entrepreneurs know launching a business is a crapshoot—and an expensive one at that. That chilling reality would scare the hell out of most of us. For an entrepreneur, it beats a roller-coaster ride any day.

No question about it, entrepreneurs are nuts. You have to be in order to walk that kind of tightrope day in and day out. They're also rule breakers, iconoclasts, and free thinkers. In short, creative mavericks on their own special wavelengths.

Are you a budding entrepreneur? Think about it.

Let's pick up the job search and retire another tired dinosaur—the résumé. There's a much better way to get your foot in the door.

JUNK YOUR RÉSUMÉ

Hiring a worker from a résumé is like trying to hire a ball player from his bubblegum card. GENE PERRET
Funny Business (1990)

I know what you're thinking. How dare I question the résumé, an institution as sacred as motherhood, the American flag—even a McDonald's Big Mac. It's blasphemy plain and simple. Why on earth do they give lunatics like me book contracts? Has the world gone stark raving mad?

Not by a long shot. Hear me out. No matter how outrageous it sounds, the disquieting truth is *résumés no longer work* for most job hunters. And they're especially bad for fiftyish job searchers who've had several jobs.

I even wrote an entire myth-busting book surrounding the résumé called *Résumés Don't Get Jobs: The Realities and Myths of Job Getting.* If you still don't believe me, read Robert Hochheiser's *Throw Away Your Résumé.* In 183 pages, Hochheiser says résumés don't work and they're the "worst way to sell your services."

Résumés produce immediate results for maybe 5 percent of job hunters—and that's being generous. But those fortunate job hunters either have perfect backgrounds (they held fast-track jobs in high-demand industries) or simply happen to be in the right place at the right time. Most of us aren't that lucky, because our work histories consist of an odd assortment of related jobs. In *Funny Business,* humorist Gene Perret summed up the résumé this way: "About all one can tell from a résumé is that the author either owns a typewriter (or computer) or knows someone who does."

So why do we persist in writing résumés? Simply, it's a tradition and such old habits are hard to break. The résumé has been elevated to an unquestioned part of the job-hunting routine. It goes part and parcel with getting a spiffy new suit and haircut and boasting a positive attitude. The thinking is: Unless your mom or dad runs the company, no employer will talk to you unless you have a résumé.

Blame it on human nature, but the fact is change doesn't come easy. History is full of incredible examples. Before Columbus set the record straight with his round-world theory, nobody questioned the flat-world paradigm. Sail too far the wrong way and you'll fall right off the face of the earth. A lot of intelligent folks actually believed that. Or what about the classic Ptolemaic versus Copernican models of the universe? For over 13 centuries, astronomer Claudius Ptolemy's theory reigned: The sun revolved around the earth. Then Copernicus proved him wrong in 1600. "Get a grip on reality," he may have snapped. "That's not the way the universe works. The earth actually revolves around the sun." A revolutionary concept for sure.

The same rigid thinking applies to the résumé. If you think I'm a lone wolf fighting an impossible battle, listen to what Jim Challenger, president of a respected Chicago outplacement firm, has to say about the résumé: "Still heralded as the key to winning a job, the résumé is today's number-one deterrent to getting a job. Many rely on the résumé as an almost sacred tool and expect it to do everything for them in the job search. It never did and never will, especially now, with large numbers of job seekers competing for far fewer jobs."

WHADDAYA MEAN, RÉSUMÉS DON'T WORK?

Before I continue debunking the résumé, a little history. For over 70 years, résumés landed job searchers interviews. By the late 1980s, they were all but useless. It's all because the world changed. Technology gave us high-speed communication linking practically every crevice of the world and creating a "global marketplace." Tack on fierce competition for markets among the industrial powers, and matters grew worse. America, once the world's standard bearer and trendsetter, lost its foothold. Japan sprinted past, ascending as technology's superstar. Japanese companies were efficient and productive, while their American counterparts wallowed in mediocrity and inefficiency. The writing on the wall couldn't be clearer: Cut costs and improve efficiencies or perish. As a result, payrolls were cut with a vengeance. Welcome to the 1980s, the decade that gave us *downsizing*, the sterile buzzword for mass firings.

You get the picture. With millions of people chasing fewer jobs, the résumé suddenly became an inefficient interview-capturing tool. But try to tell this to job searchers, especially people like you who've worked for one company for 20-plus years. Reading about the brave new world in *Time* or *Newsweek* as you sit safe and secure behind an old mahogany desk on the twenty-fifth floor of a *Fortune* 500 company offers a new reality that's hard to relate to. Dealing with it firsthand is a sobering truth that's hard to accept.

Not More Résumé Books

To make matters worse, there's nobody out there waving flags to tell you that résumés don't work and job getting isn't what it was when you were hired back in the 1960s. It has to be confusing, especially when you find an entire section of a bookstore selling résumé guides. There are—are you ready?—about 70 résumé books in print and at least 25 to 30 more in the works.

Don't think the profit-hungry publishing industry will stop peddling these consistent revenue earners. Churning out résumé books is good business. Selling books is no different from hawking candy bars or toys. Barring a catchy title like *Knock 'Em Dead Résumés!*, it's not as if one résumé book is radically different from the next. How many ways can anyone explain the difference between a chronological and a functional résumé?

More Proof, You Say?

I'm not through. Since we're fighting crowd mentality, I've got some more to say about the résumé before laying out a far better alternative. As the market grows more competitive and companies continue to pare ranks, not only are job seekers churning out more résumés; they're going to incredible lengths to get them written and distributed to prospective employees.

If all the résumé books aren't bad enough, lazy job searchers can buy easy-to-use résumé-writing software programs. Just fill in the spaces and, voilà, instant résumé. If that's a hassle, the Yellow Pages are full of résumé-writing services that will do the job for you. They tout themselves as specialists—professional résumé writers, if you can believe it. (What's next, a degree in résumé writing?) They promise a résumé that will bring results. Most of these folks are either hacks or quacks, or both.

One résumé-writing company in Shawnee, KS, charges clients

between $500 and $1000 to write their résumés. For an additional charge, the outfit will mass-mail the résumé to potential employers from a database of 10 million names. One job searcher spent $8000 to blanket the country with 10,000 résumés. The mass-mailing produced 14 interviews, but no jobs. The only ones profiting from this technique are the heads of these services. Last year, the Shawnee company grossed $3 million. You've heard of junk mail. Now there are junk résumés.

Outplacement specialist Challenger advises job seekers to avoid mass-mailing résumés. He estimates a return of only 1 to 2 percent, making it a monumental waste of time and money.

Still, other eager job hunters are faxing résumés. For many, the fax has become what the word processor was 10 years ago—a tool for quickly getting a résumé into an employer's hands. Job searchers would think twice about the fax method, however, if they knew over-burdened employers were scrapping these messages as soon as they popped out of the machine. Many annoyed employers, deluged with faxed résumés, are getting revenge by pulling the plug on their machines. Why waste expensive fax paper on résumés that will be trashed anyway?

The newest rage is sending résumés electronically. There's even a new term for it, *electronic networking.* And would you believe a brand new résumé book, *Electronic Résumés for the New Job Market (Résumés That Work for You 24 Hours a Day),* tells you how to write an electronic résumé so it can be easily read by a computer and incorporated into a job bank database available to employers who are looking for job candidates? There are plenty of job banks, catering to all professions and specialties. The trick to writing an electronic résumé is knowing which words trip the computer best. (Depending upon the job, employers have favorite words for their computers to routinely search.)

It sounds impressive, but once again, all you're doing is succumbing to the herd instinct. You're killing yourself trying to design a résumé that will stand out in a database. It reminds me of a massive Broadway cattle call in which thousands of actors audition for a single role. Some of them may have star potential, but if they don't stand out from the crowd, they won't be noticed. The same rationale applies to the electronic résumé. Yours is one of hundreds, maybe thousands, of résumés that, hopefully, will stand out in someone's database. Naturally, database and job bank advocates—usually, owners or promoters of the related services—advise job searchers to list themselves with several electronic databases for broad exposure.

What's next? If this keeps up, desperate job searchers will be stuffing their résumés into corporate ventilation systems on the remote chance they will miraculously blow on to an employer's desk.

If you're saying to yourself, "There's got to be a better way," you're right. I'm going to tell you about it soon.

THE BIRTH OF THE GENERIC RÉSUMÉ: PACKAGING BAD TASTE

Will résumé madness ever end? Only when everyone stops turning out the dumb things. With all these newfangled résumé-producing methods, you'd think we'd come across some incredible résumés— innovative, creative, award winners. Not on your life. What we have is mediocrity that's driving many employers and human resources people to drink. All that is being turned out by sophisticated résumé machinery are résumés that look and sound the same. Hence, the *generic résumé*.

It doesn't matter if the type, layout, and paper are different, if the language, approach, and content vary a little from applicant to applicant.

How any employer could spot individuality, uniqueness, and superstar qualities is beyond me. Most résumés belong in one of two categories. The first I call the Conformist (or Wonder Bread) résumé. Other than changes in name, career history, and personal information, the résumé has the same feeling, tone, and language as millions of others in circulation. The writer's goal is to be the perfect applicant, just like the zillions of other hungry job seekers. With a résumé like this, it's not hard figuring out the odds of being picked from the crowd.

At the other end of the spectrum is the Rebel résumé, put together by a writer convinced that the way to attract attention is by being outrageous and unique. Some of these résumés are award winners for breaking every résumé rule in the book. That's the good part. The bad part is they're so blatantly inappropriate, tactless, and offensive that it's doubtful these applicants will ever capture interviews, no less jobs.

In fact, I collect résumés like these, hoping to get enough to publish a book called *The 100 Most Offensive Résumés Ever Written*.

It's a guaranteed best-seller. One résumé I've saved epitomizes bad taste. On three pages, the job applicant summarized his whole life. He even included three photos of himself at different ages. In two of them, he's bare-chested (very macho) and, in the third, he looks like he just stepped off a hippie commune, circa 1968. That's not all. The résumé contains more than you ever wanted to know about the applicant. For example, he disappointed his parents by not becoming a lawyer, his girlfriend's name is Jess (short for Jessica), he's a clean-cut kind of guy who couldn't be kicked out of a group of altar boys, and his goal in life is to achieve the impossible and climb the highest mountains he can find. No joke. The pity is he's a smart man who could be unemployed for the rest of his life if he doesn't wise up and ditch his résumé.

Finally, it's mind-boggling when you consider how many résumés contain totally irrelevant information. Robert Half, author of *How to Get a Better Job in This Crazy World,* has been collecting résumé bloopers for over 40 years. Here are a few of his classics:

PERSONAL: I'm married with nine children. I don't require prescription drugs.

PERSONAL: My mother lives with me; she is a CPA and can travel.

PERSONAL: I had two children by my first wife; both live with me. She also had two kids by her second husband. My second, and present, wife had one child by each of her first two husbands and we had two kids together—all of those living with us, making a total of six. But my wife is now pregnant with twins.

QUALIFICATIONS: I am a man filled with passion and integrity and I can act on short notice. I'm a class act and do not come cheap.

I could reel off plenty more horror stories, but you get the idea. The average résumé is atrocious. And that's being kind. I'd like a penny for every time an applicant uses words like these: impacted, implemented, empowered, utilized, growth-oriented, maximize, high-visibility, extensive, challenging.

My favorite part of the résumé is the objective. Even résumé advocates admit the objective ought to be dumped. Yet millions of job searchers insist on putting this annoying one-liner at the top, immediately souring the reader. An employer has barely digested 14 words before concluding, "I hate this person."

The objective is supposed to tell readers precisely what kind of job the applicant wants. Objectives, like generic résumés, are just a bunch of hollow words. Here are a few lifted from actual résumés (maybe even yours).

- "Seeking a position which will utilize academic achievements and hands-on experience while providing for career-development opportunities."
- "A challenging and rewarding position as a sales/marketing representative."
- "Searching for a high-visibility job that affords me the opportunity to grow with the company."
- "An exciting position as a salesperson in a multinational company with opportunities to draw upon my extensive knowledge of the computer industry."
- "A fashion coordinator position in which there is room for improvement."

Had enough? Let's turn the tables. What would you do if you ran a company and received a résumé with an objective like one of those above? A rhetorical question, right? Case closed.

Now you know why résumés aren't working. The average time an employer invests in scanning résumés is 5 to 30 seconds—if you're lucky.

It would be great if all résumé-dispensing gimmicks and strategies paid off. Sadly, the effort amounts to a monumental waste of time. Hold on to your seats, here are the numbers. Companies across the country are drowning in paper. *U.S. News & World Report* estimated most *Fortune* 500 companies receive 1000 unsolicited résumés each week, and 80 percent are trashed after a cursory review. It's safe to say the average mid-size company gets between 100,000 and 300,000 résumés a year. Talk about spitting in the wind. It's easy to see why corporate recruiters are a little frazzled these days. You'd be crazy too if you had to scan hundreds of résumés daily searching for high-potential applicants.

SO IF RÉSUMÉS DON'T WORK, WHAT DOES?

A letter. In concept, it sounds simple. But preparing a great letter isn't easy. And there are no guarantees it will land you an interview.

But the good news is it's a million times better than a résumé and the odds of getting a positive response are excellent. Here's why.

- It's a complete all-in-one package, replacing résumé and cover letter.
- It's an immediate and original attention-getter. A great letter demands to be read.
- Not only does it sell you better than a résumé, it makes a more elegant and eloquent presentation.
- The letter bears your unique stamp. Rather than relying on a formula to get you in the door, you're presenting an original document, a preview of what you're all about.

Letters are especially recommended for job hoppers, career changers, and people who haven't worked for lengthy periods (such as parents returning to the work force). Rather than the perfunctory chronological résumé in which you're obliged to list the last few jobs you've had, a letter permits you to home in on critical facts and details that sell you for the specific job opening.

Despite downsizing and a topsy-turvy job market, plenty of traditional employers still frown on job hopping. Stuck in the *Father Knows Best* era, when breadwinners built lifestyles around one company, they deem job hopping as a sign of rootlessness, shiftlessness, and instability.

Think about the expression on a conservative employer's face in scanning a résumé that has an 8-year gap because the applicant waited until her two children were old enough for school before going back to work. What about the manager of a brokerage firm getting a résumé from an advertising executive with 20-plus years of experience who's now applying for a job as a broker? Would you be surprised if the manager thought the guy was nuts after digesting his résumé?

Getting back in the work force after taking a leave of absence is tough enough, but career changing, even under the best of circumstances, can be a long, hard pull. You're fighting an uphill battle with a résumé, because the outmoded job-hunting instrument is designed for people who did the same or similar things throughout their career. Career changers and, to a lesser extent, people who dropped out of the work force are rule breakers. They've left the fold. Most are in their forties; significant numbers are in their fifties and sixties. Hence, a more liberal, creative, and open-ended vehicle for presenting their skills is needed. The letter perfectly fits the bill.

If you're uptight about writing a letter, as many people are, relax. I'm going to take you through the critical steps. It's not half as painful as it sounds. It requires effort, but if you invest some time in the process, you'll be delighted with the results.

The Letter's Function

The function of the letter is to generate interest. The great part about this vehicle is it allows you to concentrate on your most salable facts—the jobs and credentials that most impress prospective employers.

A well-written letter beats the résumé at its own game by being tight, targeted, and focused. It says what has to be said and stops. Most critical, a letter is effective only if it's sent to the person who might hire you—the company owner or a high-ranking manager. *Never send a letter to a title.* You've taken a step backward. That's what a staggering number of résumé applicants all over the United States are doing. Your chances of getting a response are dismal. If you've done your homework, you've thoroughly researched the market and found companies that might value your talents. Now you're going to go for it and make the pitch of your life.

Length, Tone, and Feeling

Before you boot up your computer to write the letter of the century, let's cover the key issues. If you're thinking about writing an autobiography in letter form, forget it. If you want it to be read, rather than trashed, keep it under two pages. One and a half pages is perfect. Remember, busy employers abhor the task of hiring. They must stop whatever they're doing and rummage through stacks of résumés to find a half-dozen people with the right credentials. Make it easy for them. Give them an epistle they can digest quickly and painlessly.

Don't say you can't condense your career into a page and a half. I've done it and so have countless others.

The tone must be sincere, direct, and professional. Don't forget, there is a big difference between a personal letter and a professional letter. A personal letter has no restrictions. It can be anything you want it to be—intimate, crude, passionate, cynical, boastful, or full of slang or colloquialisms. A business letter is a whole other animal. Most important, unlike the personal letter, a professional letter distances writer and reader. It means being appropriate at all times. But it doesn't mean you can't be candid and yourself. Within the boundaries of good taste, you can write almost anything to hook your reader into summoning you for an interview. Do so by being straightforward and making your case simply, avoiding bloated adjectives, buzzwords, and empty phrases.

CRAFTING A LETTER-WRITING STYLE

As I said above, the advantage of the letter is that it homes in only on facts that best sell you. Like a reporter preparing to write a story, you must first gather all the facts and figures that ought to be included. The tough part is choosing only the most relevant material.

Now let's craft a letter. A good letter is not unlike a well-written print ad. It must capture attention, make a promise, and back that claim. These three components can be likened to a three-act play. The first act hooks the viewer on the story line, the second fleshes it out, and the third pulls everything together and works toward a conclusion. Similarly, the first part of your letter piques the reader's attention. ("This person really sounds interesting. Nobody ever asked for a job by using a letter.") The second part sells you by citing relevant jobs, and the last part concludes by asking for an interview. Simple? In concept, yes; the execution, however, requires thought and effort.

The task at hand is molding the letter to the job you're considering. Take a close look at the sample letter on the following pages.

Note how it accomplishes its goal. Attention-getting opening sentences enlist the reader's interest by making a positive connection. Before the second sentence begins, the writer has established a rapport. Just a few lines into the letter and the reader knows he or she is dealing with a seasoned professional. If a reader gets as far as the fourth sentence, the chances of reading the entire letter are excellent.

At the end of the first paragraph, the writer makes his claim: "I am offering you 28 years of sales/marketing experience in the food industry." Then he immediately backs it with some stunning credentials. Note how lean the letter is. Rather than including a chronolo-

November 23, 19XX

Ms. Irma Smartypants
Crookos Foods
2345 North Bay Highway
San Francisco, CA XXXXX

Dear Ms. Smartypants:

I learned about the opening for a marketing manager from George Crimponotski, regional manager of Loyola Foods. I've known George for almost 20 years. We met when I was marketing director of Bongo Cookies. Like George, I am a veteran of the food industry. I've watched it grow from an emerging industry of tiny mom-and-pop companies into a multibillion-dollar industry dominated by giant multinational companies. At no other time was sophisticated marketing prowess so essential. This is precisely what I'm offering you: 28 years of sales/marketing experience in the food industry.

For the past decade, I've followed your company with great interest. Crookos has a reputation for innovation. It was the first in the natural sugar-free category, and now it's jumped on the fat-free fad with a vengeance. As you well know, it takes more than incredible products to hold that position. Strategic niche marketing is what makes the difference. This is precisely the kind of expertise I can bring you. My background proves it.

As marketing director of Strikos Foods (1981–1993), I created the marketing/advertising campaign which broke its organic bread and soup line into high-end specialty shops and health food stores. In 1987, I convinced the company president Merriam Strikos to design stand-alone displays for major supermarket chains, thus avoiding crippling slotting fees. Both campaigns paid off handsomely, boosting sales 65 percent.

(Continued)

Prior to that, I was marketing coordinator at Kennicott Cracker (1973–1981), the foremost importer of English crumpets, scones, and biscuits. Initially, I was hired to build a marketing team and campaign that could open up American markets to Kennicott. Management projected the U.S. line could add 5 percent to total sales. Convincing management the figure was grossly underestimated, I created a campaign that would place the products in specialty food chains and targeted supermarkets as well. Over a 2-year period I accomplished my goal. Through a dozen hand-picked sales professionals, Americans discovered Kennicott in a big way. Its biscuit/scone line has boosted sales more than 45 percent.

In high-ranking positions at Lombardi, Ltd. and Wild & Wild, I achieved similar results.

I hold a BA degree from Stamford University and an MBA from the University of Pennsylvania's Wharton School of Business.

I've included only brief highlights of my career. At your convenience, I'd like to meet with you to tell you how I can be a valuable asset to Crookos Foods.

I will call you during the week of December 5 to arrange a mutually convenient appointment.

Sincerely,

Thomas Acquinas II

gy of jobs, he mentions only the most recent ones, because they sell him best.

Advice: Follow his lead. Stick only to facts that sell you. A résumé is a hodgepodge of meaningful and meaningless facts. A letter, on the other hand, cuts right to the chase, giving the reader a powerful sketch of a candidate's abilities.

Remember, you're competing for a busy employer's time, so be brief. Get your best punch off first with material that captures interest and forces the reader to go on.

Do not make hollow claims: "I'm a creative copywriter capable of tackling any assignment." Or, "I'm the best salesperson on the West Coast." An employer's response will be "big deal." Instead, prove you're the best by providing irrefutable accomplishments. Our letter writer doesn't come across as the messiah, just a guy who knows what he's doing.

Do not include irrelevant items such as personal details (marital status), hobbies, religion, race, philosophy, health status ("I'm in perfect health") or the ridiculous line found at the bottom of most résumés, "References furnished upon request." Are you going to tell employers to take a hike when they ask for references?

Finally, don't ever lose sight of the letter's purpose. It is a compelling sketch of you, an hors d'oeuvre whetting the reader's appetite to learn more. Say just enough to capture attention and arouse interest.

TRICKS AND TECHNIQUES FOR TURNING OUT GREAT LETTERS

Below are some helpful tips to take the pain out of preparing a letter.

1. *Rewrite and edit.* Don't expect to get it right the first time. In fact, I'd be concerned if you are satisfied with your first draft. I don't care if you're a budding Hemingway; it's impossible for a first draft to be perfect. Don't be lazy. Find a quiet place and invest time in this important task. Consider this technique: Dash off a first draft, read it over for clarity, eliminate unnecessary words, and fix your grammar. Then, put it aside for a few hours or, better yet, a day. I call this the "gestation period."

Distance yields perspective and objectivity. It's as if you're reading it for the first time. I guarantee you'll make plenty of changes and deletions.

2. *Stay focused.* Don't go off on tangents. Think before you write. Don't lose sight of your goals. Whether you're responding to a want ad, following up on a tip, or playing a hunch, position yourself so you're presenting yourself to best advantage. Don't ever assume you're the first one to make a bid for the job. Whether you're the first or fourth, try to be the best by brilliantly selling yourself.

3. *Find your own voice.* It may take a few drafts, but work toward finding a comfortable way of expressing yourself. Don't try to impress readers with big words and grandiose statements. Instead, keep the language simple and sentences short. A great letter needs no interpretation. It ought to be a quick, easy read.

4. *Keep a professional distance.* As I said before, don't overstep your bounds and become too familiar with your reader. A business letter requires a professional voice at all times.

5. *Use variations for different jobs.* You probably have one or two versions of your résumé for applying for different kinds of jobs. Use the same approach with your letter. If you're multiskilled, as are so many job hunters your age, you ought to have variations of your letter.

Say you're in advertising. Over a 25-plus-year career, you may have worked as a copywriter and an account executive. Or, if you're experienced in the computer industry, you've worked as a systems analyst, programmer, and salesperson. In the course of a three-decade career, it stands to reason you'd test different sectors of your industry. One letter wouldn't do the job, but variations on a single theme would. If you were applying for a sales job in a software company, you'd include only those positions which highlight your sales credentials. It's a far cry from a résumé which is a jumble of information.

Reading a résumé can be likened to roaming around a dusty old attic looking at scattered mementos. A letter, on the other hand, picks out only those shards of the past that best sell you. The trick is knowing the right ones. Everything employers need to know should practically jump off the page. No interpretation is required.

6. *Read the letter over carefully.* Before you bless your letter and send it off into the ozone, do one last exercise. Before you print it out, use this last-minute checklist to make sure it's "letter" perfect.

- Is it a quick, easy read?
- Do opening sentences capture a reader's attention?
- Is it tight and targeted, avoiding buzzwords, bizspeak, colloquialisms, and slang?
- Is it grammatically correct?
- Are there spelling errors? Word of caution. If you use a computer and your software has a spellcheck feature, take advantage of it. But don't accept it as gospel. Names must still be double-checked. What could be more embarrassing than misspelling the name of the person you're asking for a job? Think about the impression that makes.
- How is the presentation? Is it neat and clean? You don't have to use expensive rag bond stationery or fancy type. Sturdy white stationery and standard fonts will do just fine. Anything else is pretentious and unnecessary. But it must be spotless. One smudge can kill it all for you.

Finally, read the letter over one more time, *word by word,* to make sure a tiny error didn't slip through. Sign it, send it off, and cross your fingers. Keep a record of all letters sent so you can follow up at the appropriate time. If you did your job well, you may be pleasantly shocked to get a call within a week summoning you for an interview.

What better time to rev up for the hot seat and find out how to turn in the interview performance of your life?

INTERVIEW TRAPS, NO-NOS, AND POINTERS

You're up at bat. You scored with your letter and you were summoned for an interview. Naturally, you're nervous, uptight, scared, petrified—maybe all of the above.

There is nothing profound to say about the interview other than that it's still a nerve-wracking experience. For good reason. Bomb it and you won't get the job. What could be clearer? It's easy to see why applicants, ages 18 to 80, get uptight when sitting in the hot seat. And it's no wonder comics have poked fun at the job interview for years. In *Funny Business,* humorist Gene Perret writes:

You know it's going to be a tough interview when...

...the interviewer wears military boots, a monocle, and carries a swagger stick.

...you're escorted into the interviewer's office by the company chaplain.

...the interviewer offers you a cup of coffee? a cigarette? a blindfold?

Lighten up. The interview is not the end of the world. The worst that can happen is you blow it. I don't say that to be flip. But I'm somewhat of a fatalist when it comes to evaluating the impact of critical events. It's as basic as you'll get the job if it was meant to happen. And if you don't, you either don't belong there or maybe ought to go back to the drawing board and scrutinize your performance under a microscope. My attitude doesn't mean you shouldn't give it your all; it just takes the tension level down a few notches so you can do your very best.

A little levity doesn't hurt either. Some distance and objectivity from the pending event can help you turn in an award-winning performance. Let's get in shape so you can impress the hell out of your interviewer.

Before we look at the phases of the interview process, here's some advice about a critical, yet often overlooked, first step.

GETTING IN SHAPE FOR THE BIG EVENT

Of course you're going to research the company. Pros like yourselves know this. So why even mention it? It's because a lot of lazy folks out there just assume their beauty, charm, and effervescent personalities will carry the show. Catch the next SST back from Oz pronto. If you've landed an interview, you have to realize there are no shortcuts to job getting. It takes hard work, time, and creativity. So don't make short shrift of these all-important steps. You can see the finish line from here. Don't slacken your pace.

Preparation is a two-phase process: (1) learning all you can about the company and (2) jotting down only those facts and figures that best sell you for the job.

A little homework wouldn't hurt. When researching companies, go beyond the quick snapshots offered by Standard & Poor's or Dun & Bradstreet. Spend time in the library checking out news clips from business and trade magazines. Find out if your library subscribes to Infotrak, the neat software that instantly accesses newspaper or magazine stories on a host of subjects.

Know more than just the basics about the companies you're pursuing. You'll make a strong impression if you walk in knowing about new product launches or pending acquisitions.

To tune up for the event, pull out all the accomplishments and skills that prove you're amply qualified. The letter whetted the reader's appetite with a sampling of your accomplishments. Face to face, you need to round out the picture with specific details and events.

Let's get ready for the hot seat.

THE UGLY TRUTH ABOUT INTERVIEWS

Interviews are tough for everyone, but they're particularly hard for you because of a glaring strike against you: *your age.* Don't be depressed or angry about it. Just take it as a given and be prepared to deal with it. I don't mean walking into the interview with a nasty attitude ready to do battle. You know where that'll take you. Also, don't feel so defeated and burned out that you'll grab any crumb thrown your way.

If you want to win, straighten out your attitude. Be prepared to walk into a potential minefield. Rather than being treated like a relic from the Paleolithic period, you'll be greeted with respect and deference. Incredible!

The only attitude to exhibit is one of total control and self-composure. Compare yourself to a professional basketball player walking onto the court for a playoff game. As soon as the athlete is spotted, the crowd applauds. They sense his power, control, confidence, and strength. This is what you must convey. It's the first step in making a great first impression. Your attitude reveals how you feel about yourself. If that feeling is positive, you'll be confident and upbeat, transmitting self-confidence from every pore.

THE LIVE-OR-DIE FIRST 5 MINUTES

The fun begins as soon as you walk through the door and the interviewer claps eyes on you. Like it or not, you've already been scrutinized, dissed, dismissed, or accepted. You haven't even said a word and the interviewer has formed a picture of you on the basis of how you carry yourself, shake hands, and dress. Bomb during these critical minutes and you'll never play in that town again. The interviewer will take you through the interview routine, but trust me, you've struck out. It doesn't matter what you say.

Unfair you think? Not at all. Maybe you were once on the other side of the desk and hired your fair share of people over the years. How important was that initial impression and what did you look for in an applicant? *Answer:* The first impression was critical. I guarantee you looked for a well-rounded package that knocked your socks off by looking and sounding good.

According to humorist Perret, President Lincoln once turned down a person recommended for a position because he didn't like his face. Even back then, first impressions could make or break you. More recently, Lee Iacocca, Chrysler's savior and the father of the Ford Mustang, said in his autobiography, "I learned to figure people out pretty quickly. To this day, I can usually tell a fair amount about somebody from our first meeting."

In *The First Five Minutes*, Norman King describes those pivotal early minutes:

> By the time the second hand has traveled five times around your wristwatch, two things will have happened. You will have decided exactly how much you trust or distrust your business acquaintance and, likewise, the other person will have decided exactly how much he or she trusts or distrusts you.

Let's look at the components of that snapshot closely.

1. *Dress.*   You've heard the cliché "Clothes make the man (or woman)." When I was an angry college kid, my eyes crossed when anyone said that to me. Now, after knocking around the job market for three decades, I nod my head in agreement. We all have to grow up sooner or later. The simple truth is if you want to get anywhere in the organizational world, you'd better look the part. An interviewer sees a well-dressed man or woman and immediately concludes: "Here's someone who takes good care of him- or herself." It may not be true, but that's the impression it creates.

Conservative is the command word when it comes to wardrobe. You don't want to look like you stepped out of the 1960s and you don't want to go overboard with the trendy designer stuff either. Avoid extremes. It's okay to be current and appropriately "cool," but don't overdo it. I won't say look your age, because I have no idea what that means. But I will caution you against trying to go toe to toe with Generation X.

Suits, preferably in black, gray, or blue, convey professionalism. Rather than casual matching pants and sports jacket, men should stick to formal business suits. The same goes for women, although stylish businesslike dresses will do fine. Ties? Try conservative blues, muted reds, and Ivy League stripes. Avoid wild or day-glo colors.

Here's some quick dress tips for men: No frayed cuffs or sloppy-looking shirts. Shoes ought to be polished to a high sheen. Believe it or not, well-polished shoes convey a powerful image. Socks ought to be long so that legs don't show.

For women, wearing stockings with runs or boots instead of shoes makes a terrible impression. Understated jewelry ought to complement the outfit.

Absolute no-nos: Missing buttons, clothing or tie stains, jackets that don't close, and outfits that look thrown together earn demerits on the first-impression scale.

2. *Personal grooming.* Women's makeup should be subtle. Chipped nail polish or roots showing through on dyed hair make a terrible impression.

Men's hair should be neat and combed. Note that shoulder-length hair and pony tails don't fly in most conservative midwestern companies. If you're out to make a statement with your hair, be prepared to suffer the consequence of indefinite unemployment.

3. *Eye contact.* Don't look at the floor, the ceiling, or out the window. Easy and relaxed eye contact, as opposed to menacing or anxious, is what's needed. Like they say, eyes are the window to the soul. Many job searchers make the mistake of trying to outstare the interviewer. Remember, you're there to impress the hell out of this person, not win a staring contest.

4. *Handshake.* I've met men, even a couple of women, who've come close to breaking bones when shaking my hand. Although a limp, wishy-washy handshake makes a bad impression, so does the "I'm as powerful as Arnold Schwarzenegger" variation. A firm, quick, and confident handshake will do.

5. *Posture, voice, and energy level.* How you carry yourself is also important. You don't have to stand and sit like a marine, but you must keep your back straight, square your shoulders, and avoid slouching in your chair.

Be aware of how you sound. Consider how nerve-wracking it is listening to a screamer, shouter, mumbler, or whisperer. Most people have no idea how they really sound. It may not be a bad idea to record your voice to find out how you come across. You may be shocked at the sound of your own voice. Nevertheless, it's a good way to find a level and speed that's comfortably absorbed by listeners.

A Chicago headhunter summed up the ideal interview candidate as someone who is comfortable in his or her own skin. This person has mastered the art of human interaction by presenting a balanced impression—neither overly nervous or aggressive. From the moment someone enters the room, the candidate should appear comfortable and unthreatened. Immediately, give the impression you're capable of handling any situation.

A little humor—not the crude, stand-up comic variety—wouldn't hurt either. The candidate who can crack an innocuous joke, innocently poke fun at himself, or draw a humorous aside, scores immediate points. Good-hearted, clean humor has universal appeal. Not only is it a wonderful icebreaker; it also creates a comfortable rapport, presenting you as an easygoing person who doesn't take herself too seriously.

If you can't comfortably pull off a tension-breaking one-liner, do the next best thing and try smiling, rather than looking like you're about to be strapped into the electric chair. It helps to set the stage for the bulk of the interview.

BUILDING CONNECTIONS AND RAPPORT

If you pass the initial inspection, the next hurdle is establishing rapport. This is a tricky stage that ought to be handled with utmost care. Remember, you're fighting the clock. Your fate is sealed in those critical first 5 minutes. Even if your costume and look are perfect, you won't get the job if the interviewer doesn't like you. Who said the world was fair?

The goal is not to become instant drinking buddies, but simply to find a common comfort ground that leads to the next interview stage. Here's how to do it:

1. *Let the interviewer set the pace.*   The interviewer is not unlike the director of a film or play. He or she makes the rules and sets the pace. Your job is to play your role to this person's specifications. So hang back and let the director set the stage. From the onset, understand and respect the power structure. The interviewer controls the event.

2. *Speak when spoken to.*   If you encounter nerve-wracking silences in the beginning, deal with them. Don't, however, feel compelled to fill them. Some interviewers may be testing you to see if you have the composure and self-control to deal with silence. Others may just be shy people who are getting comfortable themselves. Whatever the reason, relax and don't run off at the mouth because you're nervous.

3. *Chitchat is the best icebreaker.*   Small talk is the best icebreaker and sets the tone for the interview. Make the most of it. Interviewers have their favorite small-talk subject. It could be the weather, traffic conditions, sports, or politics. Whatever it is, pretend to enjoy it. Hopefully, you'll be able to make a contribution to the conversation. If the interviewer starts talking about a recent basketball game and you know nothing about the sport, ad-lib.

At least be a good listener by smiling attentively and nodding in agreement. Whatever you do, don't be in any rush to change the subject and get on with the interview. That is up to the interviewer. Go with the flow, as they say. Every interviewer has a personal style. Small talk could run up to 15 minutes, accompanied by coffee or another beverage.

Whatever you do, don't underestimate this critical period. Even if you're talking about your favorite sport, remember that everything you say is being evaluated. Every stage of the interview process, even innocuous small talk, is important. The best time to size a candidate up is during talk about nonwork subjects. It's also a good time to take stock of the interviewer. In these critical moments, you'll learn whether you're dealing with Mother Teresa or Machiavelli, Hitler, and Attila the Hun all crammed into one nasty package.

Read this person right and you've got it made. Adjust to his or her rhythms and the interview will effortlessly roll along. In fact, you might even enjoy it. Take your signals from the interviewer, who'll let you know when it's time to shift gears to serious issues.

THE BIG SEGUE: LISTENING FOR CUES

The pace accelerates when the interviewer changes the tone of the meeting. Maybe it's through a gesture—the simple folding of hands—or an adjustment in tone of voice. "I could talk politics all day, Betty, but we'd better get down to the work at hand and learn more about you." At that moment, the curtain flies up and the interrogation officially begins. Get ready to sell your little heart out and prove you're the only applicant for the job.

Remember, take your cues from the interviewer. He or she has a lot of questions to ask. Your job is to return quick, terse, and articulate answers. Long, rambling answers are to be avoided at all costs. So think before you speak. Milo O. Frank, author of *How to Get Your Point Across in 30 Seconds—Or Less,* advises thinking in sound bites. According to Frank, the average person's attention span is 30 seconds. Now you know why the average time of all TV news stories is one and a half minutes. That's 30 seconds to set up the story, 30 more to spill the guts of the story, and another 30 to wrap it up.

Don't get bent out of shape over these numbers. The important message is not to waste time when making your point.

No matter how difficult or off the wall the question, don't ever forget why you're there. Your job is to convince the interviewer you're the perfect candidate for the job. Every sentence must drive home your value. The goal is to meet a need. Burton Kaplan, author of *Everything You Need to Know to Talk Your Way to Success,* said the five most powerful words in the English language are, "What's in it for me?" Whether you're asking for a raise, bigger projects, or a job, focus on addressing the what's-in-it-for-me state of mind. Says Kaplan:

> Everybody—you, your preacher, the boss, the company, friends, children, clerks, even your cat!—acts out of self-interest. We filter the world through our secret needs. If what you happen to want somehow fulfills their most pressing need at the moment, bingo— you are certain to get it. And if it doesn't, you can be just as certain you won't.

The clearer you are about what the employer wants, the easier it will be to sell yourself appropriately.

Uppermost, never promote yourself in the abstract. Never lose sight of the what's-in-it-for-me attitude. Rather than asking for a job, you're bringing the employer a gift—yourself. You're the superstar who's going to create miracles—increase productivity, capture new customers, design new services. Relentlessly address employers' needs and you've got them in the palm of your hands. If they care about the growth and health of their company, they have no choice but to hire you. Infuse all that with energy and passion and you're well on your way.

Remember this advice when searching for right answers.

PRECIOUS TIPS, SURPRISE ZINGERS

If you're lucky, employers will ask straight-on, old-fashioned questions without any hidden meanings. For example:

"Why do you want this job?"

"What can you do for us?"

"Are you willing to travel?"

"When can you start?"

But that's too simple and direct—not to mention, logical. Thanks to New Age ethics, employers search for perfect, omniscient, highly motivated candidates. They reason that the best way to get them is by asking indirect, obscure, deep, off-the-wall questions. If this keeps up, by the millennium job applicants will be interpreting Rorschach tests. If Freud were alive today, he'd be pulling down hefty retainers from *Fortune* 500 companies, maybe even grossing more than management guru/motivational speaker Tom Peters.

Through it all, remember why you're sitting in the hot seat. The idea is to return correct answers sounding the right buzzwords. It's an odd, often silly, and pretentious game. But if you want the job, you'd better learn to excel at it.

Before I list possible questions, let me offer some tips and suggestions for delivering great answers.

Evade the Age Issue

Watch out for direct or indirect questions about your age. Face it, plenty of sadistic interviewers out there—many of whom work for human resources departments—would love to make a big deal about your age. "A woman your age might have a tough time keeping up the pace." Or, "Are you sure you can put in these kinds of hours? You're not as young as you used to be." Or, "You've probably got a lot of years behind you." Or, "I bet you're not a day over 55." Although legitimately enraged, be careful and unclench your fists.

Advice: Pick your battles carefully. Think twice about going one on one over the age issue. You can straighten out this person professionally without going for the jugular. You can explain how the interviewer violated Equal Employment Opportunity Commission (EEOC) laws and you have every intention of taking legal action. According to EEOC regulations, employers are breaking the law if they ask about an applicant's age, creed, religion, race, sex, marital status, or military service. If you want the job, the smart approach is to politely evade the issue, swallow your pride, and be cool. Just drive home the fact you're capable of doing the job as well as a 25-year-old. "My past record at Bozo Widgets proves I can handle 16-hour days and 7-day schedules. More important than stamina is the quality of my work, which Mr. Bozo himself will attest to."

Also, bear in mind that many naive employers may drop an inappropriate age question with no ulterior motive. Who said all employers are intelligent? Some are trying to be cute. Others are merely making what they think is an innocent observation, unaware they're violating EEOC laws. But if you're turned off by the company or employer and have no desire to work there, say anything you want or take legal action. You've got nothing to lose. Enjoy some well-earned revenge.

Keep Politics Out of It

Avoid anything hinting at company politics or personal disputes you had at prior jobs. Prospective employers don't want to hear any of this. More important, it makes you look bad. Nobody wants an organizational screw-up, malcontent, or whistle-blower.

Advice: Keep your dirty laundry to yourself. If you have skeletons in your closet, keep them there. Some applicants have a bad habit of letting it all hang out. Their philosophy is "I have nothing to hide." That's naive. No one has an unblemished record. Smart people know what events work either for or against them. The idea is to chart a smooth course for yourself by avoiding messy issues surrounding personality disputes. Try not to say things like, "My boss thought anyone over 50 was washed up. When I asked for a promotion she turned me down, saying a bigger job would give me a coronary in 6 months." Or, "My boss fired me because I wouldn't sleep with him. Every time we were alone in the office, he had his hands all over me."

Even though an employer will listen with polite interest, you'll be branded a troublemaker as soon as you exit. "Uh oh, I smell trouble. God forbid, I should say the wrong thing and I'll be slapped with a lawsuit."

Take the hint. Don't put yourself in a position where you have to defend your actions. Remember, you're there to sell yourself into a job. Nothing more! If you don't have anything positive to say, don't say anything at all.

The Seven Questions Interviewers Love to Ask

Now for some questions you can expect. First, here are seven easy questions employers love to ask.

1. Why do you want to work for us?
2. What qualities do you bring to the job?
3. Why should we hire you as opposed to someone else?
4. Why did you leave your last job?
5. How far would you like to go with the company?
6. What is your long-term career goal?
7. Where else are you interviewing?

Keep all your answers short and to the point. Remember what I said about attention spans. Think before speaking and don't get enmeshed in irrelevant details. You can't go wrong delivering straight, honest, terse answers to the above questions. Remember, every answer must sell you in a positive, upbeat way, always meeting a pressing need.

For example, when asked why you want to work for a company, avoid flag-raising generalities about the company's great reputation. Instead, offer specific reasons. For instance, "Over the past 5 years, your company has dominated the office market with a host of revolutionary new products. I can make a significant contribution to the marketing of these new products." Your answer should show that you made an effort to learn about the organization and its problems plus offer a thoughtful examination of how your talents might be of use.

Avoid opening up a can of worms when asked about your last job. If it was corporate politics or your boss hated your guts and fired you because he was a manic-depressive alcoholic subject to paranoid episodes, simply say, "There was a massive cost-cutting reorganization. Upper management eliminated most of middle management. Since I didn't have the seniority some of the managers enjoyed, I was among the first to go." How's that for an innocuous answer? Never forget the undiluted truth can do irreparable harm.

INTERVIEW TRAPS TO AVOID

Some annoying interview areas just won't go away. Here are 11 interview traps to watch out for.

1. *Tell me about yourself.* I'm sure employers have tossed this at you before. Don't make too big a deal out of it. The interviewer is asking for concrete facts in a vague way. He or she wants pertinent, convincing information that you're the person for the job. Needless to say, she doesn't want to know what you had for breakfast, what you do on weekends, or your opinions about downsizing. The interviewer wants to know about your accomplishments relating to the job you seek. You're also being tested to see how well you communicate and how fast you think on your feet.

2. *Why should we hire you?* Now is your chance to do some big-time grandstanding. Twenty years ago, you'd have returned a lot of gobbledygook about the search for growth, security, and a rewarding career track. Now you can lay it on the line and spell out precisely what you can do for this employer. Tie your goals to those of your employer's.

Again, never stop selling bottom-line benefits to prospective employers. Drive home the fact that knowledge accumulated over a 25-plus-year career is priceless. Employers would have to be out of their minds not to take advantage of it. The point you're making is that you have a knack for being one step ahead of the times.

3. *Where do you see yourself 10 years from now?* "Who the hell knows? Maybe 8 feet under." Another dumb one. Whatever you do, don't reel off the first answer that pops into your head. Any employer on top of the times knows that most workers change jobs every few years. Nevertheless, try to be realistic and pragmatic without appearing cocky. "In a couple of years, I'd like to be running the marketing division, creating programs that boost sales and open new territories. Given enough freedom and support, I'm confident I can significantly increase your profit margins." That's right. You're shouting the right words: Benefit! Benefit! Benefit!

4. *What would you consider an ideal job?* "Yours, Bozo!" No, don't lunge for your interviewer. You're outraged that someone with your background and experience would be asked such a dumb question. Knock the person's socks off by coming back with: "I doubt if there is a perfect job, Mr. Peabrain. The best you can do is try to

come as close to it as possible. An almost perfect job is one in which you're doing something you enjoy and seeing positive results at the same time. Hence, both worker and company are benefiting from the relationship." Yes, indeed. Once again, you drove home benefit.

5. *Tell me about your strengths and weaknesses.*   I'm sure you've been asked this one before. It's another trap. Whatever you do, don't give equal weight to your strengths and weaknesses. Eighty-five percent of your answer should center around your strengths, which must be highlighted with facts. Don't say you're innovative and creative. Prove you are by citing specifics. What programs, projects, and systems have you developed? What did they mean for the company in terms of productivity, market share, the bottom line?

Even though honesty may be a major strength, don't ever discuss a serious weakness. Instead, mention something insignificant that's actually a strength disguised as a minor weakness. For example, you're a perfectionist who won't give up on a problem until it's solved. Or you tend to expect too much of subordinates and are disappointed when they don't deliver.

Warning: What you consider a small fault, an interviewer may consider serious. For instance, saying you have no patience for inefficiency could be perceived as being intolerant or hot-tempered. Be careful.

6. *What were the best and worst aspects of your last job?*   Watch out. This one could explode if not handled properly. Certainly, there were aspects of prior jobs you hated. You wouldn't be normal if you loved every part of your job. Nevertheless, don't dwell on negatives. Remember, many human resources types are gunning for older workers. They're looking for reasons to knock you out of the race and label you as a set-in-your-ways, never satisfied, grumpy old curmudgeon.

Describe bad experiences as positive steps in your development. For example, because the company had an entrenched bureaucracy, you learned to develop constructive techniques to get things done quickly. Negatives should be used as opportunities demonstrating how you were aggressive and determined to realize your goals. Employers want to hear how you approached and overcame difficult challenges.

7. *How do you spend your free time?*   Don't say it's at the racetrack or O'Ryan's Pub hoisting boilermakers. Here's yet another zinger question. It's perfectly okay to talk about your favorite sports or hobbies, but it's more important to say you make time to do considerable reading to stay current with your field. If the opening arises, cite books or articles you've recently read. "I loved Reg Dingo's observations about the virtual workplace in *Our Virtual Future.* We're less than a decade away from that reality, Ms. Porpoise Toad-Farling."

8. *You've had quite a number of jobs in the past two decades. How do I know you'll stick around?*   Nobody said all employers read *Fortune, Forbes,* and *Nation's Business.* If they did, they'd know job hopping is no longer a black mark, but a survival tactic. Drive this point home politely and matter-of-factly, without going through the messy details of each job change. Dwell on reorganizations, mergers, cost-cutting efforts, and spritz the "downsizing" word around a bit. The interviewer will quickly see the big picture: You had no choice in the matter.

9. *What are some of the major accomplishments in your life?* Here's a variation on the old "What is the meaning of life?" question. Again, always remember that no matter how far afield a question seems, your job is to bring it back to the reason you're there. If this question is handled creatively, fiftyish workers can turn it to their advantage by citing landmark firsts in their career. For example, your first raise, promotion, or breakthrough project, or possibly a team-building job producing impressive results. The idea is to mention an important event, what you learned, and of course, what it meant for the company. Again, sell Benefit! Benefit! Benefit!

As an added touch, without getting maudlin or messy, why not mention a couple of your personal turning points which gave meaning and essence to your life. Examples: Marrying Margaret, your beloved wife of 20-plus years and raising three darling little brats, Maggie, Marty, and Morticia, who just happened to win full scholarships to Yale, Harvard, and Tufts. Don't make too much of the personal stuff. Presenting yourself as a solid citizen who loves his family and respects the Big Mac can't help but add a point or two.

10. *Speaking self-analytically, would you say you have a competitive nature?*   Employers want workers who have a healthy attitude toward competition, yet don't come across as mercenaries. Admitting you have a competitive nature means you will work hard and fight for something you believe in or want (a promotion, project, new territory, sales quota).

11. *What kind of money are you looking for?*   Be careful. This one can come back to haunt you if it's answered incorrectly. It's safe to assume you already know the salary range. You wouldn't be there if the money wasn't right. The question is premature and should not be asked before a job offer is made. (More on salary negotiating strategies in the next chapter.) The best answer to salary questions is a polite cop-out. "The official salary range is in the right ballpark, Ms. Trickyslick." Leave it at that.

You get the idea. I'm sure plenty more oddball questions exist for interviewers to ask. Walk in prepared to field all questions and you won't be taken by surprise. Even if a question seems off the wall, there is probably a job-related nucleus to it. Think first before answering.

When the interviewer winds down with the last question, the interview is not over. Now it's your turn to fire some questions at the interviewer.

YOUR TURN AT BAT

Getting up to leave after the interviewer has asked the last question is a big mistake that could cost you the job. To make a lasting, positive impression, ask some intelligent questions. The lead-in should sound something like, "Well, that's about it, Mr. Dahmer. Is there anything you'd like to know about Tasty Bones, Inc.?"

Absolutely. And you have no intention of letting the interviewer off the hook either. You just happen to have a number of questions you'd like to fire away.

Thoughtful questions present you as a serious candidate who's not about to settle for any job that comes along. Instead, you intend to find one that meets your criteria.

Here are 11 questions you might ask:

1. What is the principal job of this department?
2. Could you describe my job in detail? (A five-line job description never fully explains a job. Make no assumptions about what you're going to be doing. Ask. When it's laid out in front of you, you may not like it.)
3. What is the most important responsibility?

4. What kind of person do you want? (Nothing like a little surprise honesty. I doubt if they're prepared for this one.)

5. Where are the last couple of people who held this job? (If they're in prison or a psycho ward, make a speedy exit.)

6. To whom would I report?

7. Who are the other people I will work with?

8. Where will I work? (Don't assume you'll get a posh carpeted corner office complete with open bar and stereo. Ask. You may be very disappointed.)

9. What is the work schedule? How flexible is it?

10. What about bonuses, profit sharing, health insurance, vacations, perks?

11. Are there any learning opportunities? (Many small companies have incredible learning opportunities, including affiliations with local universities or colleges.)

That's just a sampling. There may be other questions relevant to your particular industry or skill. If you're concerned about any aspect of the job, no matter how piddling, this is the time to get it off your chest. By now, the interviewer is exhausted and praying you'll go home. However, after a question barrage like the one above, there is no way he or she won't leave impressed.

When it's all over, it wouldn't hurt to take an objective look at your interview performance to see how you did.

EVALUATE YOUR INTERVIEW PERFORMANCE

If you screwed up, don't feel sorry for yourself. Rather than see it as a lost opportunity, look at what you've learned. The idea is not to make the same mistakes—if indeed you made any—again.

The best time to scrutinize your performance is within 10 hours of the interview. Don't wait until the next day. Go over the event while it's fresh in your mind. Take the following evaluation questionnaire and write down your answers. Be brutally honest with yourself. No one is going to see this but you.

Evaluation Questionnaire

1. Did you answer questions directly and tersely?
2. Did you include too many extraneous details?
3. Did you wander from the subject?
4. What kind of tone did you use? Was it authoritative? hesitant? inconsistent? confident?
5. What about the speed at which you spoke? Was it too slow? too fast? just right?
6. Did you maintain eye contact with the interviewer?
7. Did you fidget with your hands or were they still in your lap?
8. Did you sit upright in your chair, as opposed to slouching?

How did you do? As I said, if you made some miserable faux pas, here's an opportunity to perfect your act.

Let's move on and talk money. You've impressed the hell out of the employer. Now the company's going to try and get you as cheaply as possible. Stick with me. I'm going to show you how to get what you want—without compromising.

CHAPTER

TWENTY

"PAY ME A DECENT SALARY OR I WALK!"

Things are looking up. A company is interested in hiring you. People there are impressed by your background, experience, and attitude. More important, they think you can make money for them. If you're lucky, they'll pay you what you're worth. More realistically, they'll try to get you cheap. After all, why pay more than they have to? From this point, the game only gets more interesting.

Let's run through the critical events till now. Everything has fallen into place nicely. All the time and effort you've channeled into your job search has paid off. Your letter was great and you handled yourself like a pro during the interview. When they tossed out the zinger salary question—"What kind of money are you looking for?"—you had the good sense to leave the subject wide open by stating a pay range, rather than pinning yourself down to a specific amount. It proved a smart tactic. The only time to get serious about money is when a company has decided you're the one and has made you a job offer. The scene shifts when the employer says something like, "Nancy, we're very impressed with you. We think you can make some incredible contributions at New Age Bombs, Inc. We're prepared to offer you a salary of $65,000 a year. Would that be acceptable?"

No, you're not going to grab this weasel by the neck and scream at the top of your lungs, "No, it's not acceptable, you sniveling little runt. How dare you offer me an insulting salary that's less than I earned on my last job? You know what you can do with your salary and job offer?"

Instead, you're going to smile coolly and, with utmost composure, spout something like, "I'm flattered you think me qualified and I'm excited about the prospect of working at New Age Bombs. However, the salary you offered is considerably less than I anticipated. Actually, it's 25 percent less than I was paid at Perfect Cannons.

157

I'd like to discuss this with you further. I'm sure we can come to a mutually agreeable figure."

OPERATE FROM A POSITION OF STRENGTH

Excellent. Let's give our imaginary applicant a big hand for coming back with a brilliant, deftly delivered answer. There's no way she's going to walk away with less than she deserves.

Sadly, most job applicants—even experienced folks like you—blow this critical phase for two big reasons. First, they're uncomfortable talking about money. Oddly, money remains an awkward subject. You've heard the expression, "Money brings out the worst in a person." Blame it all on the bad press that money has received over the years. The New Testament condemned the green stuff: "The love of money is the root of all evil." Neo-Freudian Sandor Ferenczi equated money with body wastes. You get the idea. The harsh reality is, just try to get along without it. Ironically, most of us spend 50 to 60 hours a week working for money, yet we're uptight talking about it.

If you've got a problem getting maximum money for yourself, think about the role money plays in your life and you won't be as timid talking about it. Money remains one of the keys to life. Money spells power in billboard-size letters. It is the ultimate door opener. The more you make, the better your standard of living. Long ago, you discovered that money is the ultimate scorecard. Would it be wrong admitting you want to earn more than your neighbor? Buy that better car, bigger house, expensive college education for your kids. Hell, wanting the best is as American as apple pie and the flag rolled into one.

Truth be told, I admit I love the neat toys money can buy. And I'm sure you do too. So have no hesitation about wheeling and dealing for it. After all, employers aren't giving anything away. They're just buying what you have to sell. Don't sell yourself short.

Second, many fiftyish applicants feel they must settle because of their age. "Since I'm getting on in years, I'd better be realistic and take whatever is offered. After all, I don't have that many good years left." Why not open the window and jump right now? If you think that way, I guarantee you'll be shortchanged and miserable to boot. If anything I've said sank in, you ought to be quietly outraged that anyone has the chutzpah to offer you less than you deserve. To help you get it, remember the following four lessons.

LESSON 1.   Don't lose your cool. Walk into a salary negotiation prepared to encounter anything, especially the age issue. But don't be paranoid about it either. Wait and see what happens.

LESSON 2.   Don't undersell yourself. By now, you know what your strengths are. You're an unparalleled pro and no one can convince you otherwise. Don't be intimidated by competition 10 and 20 years your junior.

LESSON 3.   Know what you're worth. The demand for different skills fluctuates yearly. Take engineers, for example. One year, chemical engineers are hot; the next, they're out of favor. Yet there's a constant demand for advanced computer, financial, and accounting skills. Find out what big and small companies are paying for your particular talent.

LESSON 4.   Don't inflate your last salary. If the thought never even occurred to you, jump to the next section. The truth is, doctoring prior salaries has become the rule rather than the exception. And the situation has gotten worse. About a year ago, a respected headhunter was quoted in *The Wall Street Journal* with an estimate that 95 percent of all Americans overstate their compensation at one time or other. He went on to say the practice has gotten out of control.

Warning: Back in the old days, you stood an excellent chance of getting away with an inflated figure, because few companies verified salaries. Not any more. Employers know they can get the cream of the crop and they'll go to all ends to ensure this. Applicants, junior to senior, are often checked out thoroughly. References are called and pay history is verified. Many employers are asking for W-2 income forms to verify prior salaries. It's not a very elegant or diplomatic approach, but if you've been burned once, you'll take every precaution necessary.

Don't ask for trouble. Operate from a position of strength by playing it straight. It sounds corny, but honesty is the best policy.

THE FINE ART OF SALARY NEGOTIATION

Salary negotiation is neither fun nor easy. Although it could be a breeze, realistically, you'll probably have to sweat some to get what you want.

Whatever you do, don't rush the process. Just as you had the good sense to let your interviewer control the show, do the same now. Show you're anxious to get the money conversation over with quickly and you'll be backed into a corner before you know what's happening.

If it's a small company, there's a good chance interviewer and employer are one in the same, making the negotiation process easier. Since you already established a rapport with this person, you know what to expect. So relax and let the employer make the first move. Take your cues from him or her. Salary negotiation is a subtle dance between employer and applicant.

In the best negotiations, there are no winners or losers. Both parties walk away feeling like they got exactly what they want. A common chord has been struck.

Beware of High-Pressure Tactics

Nevertheless, be prepared for high-pressure tactics and the take-it-or-leave-it strategy. To get the process over with quickly and intimidate the hell out of you at the same time, many employers present the salary as a fait accompli. They make it clear that if you don't want it, plenty of other qualified applicants would jump at it. It's a tired tactic that unfailingly works. Don't let it hoodwink you, no matter how much you want the job. Look at the facts and you'll see they're playing with your head.

No matter what employers say, the one thing they want to avoid is going back to the drawing board and negotiating with new applicants. The salary negotiating process is just as painful for them as it is for you. You both want to resolve it and get to work. If it means paying you more to make you happy, usually they'll reluctantly do so. However, count on being put through the ringer before they agree to it. Remember, you're their first choice. Regardless of what they say, they will negotiate. Feel better?

Don't Give Away the House

Let's search for that happy middle ground and negotiate a deal you can accept. The employer says the range is $65,000 to $75,000, but the best the company can do is pay $70,000. If you're looking for $75,000, be realistic and settle for a salary of $73,000, which is pretty close. Or, if you're superconfident and think you can pull it off, hold out for the top salary. All we're talking about is a $2000 difference.

If you're asking for only a few thousand dollars more than the offered price, chances are the negotiation will be fast and everyone will walk away happy. However, if there is a big difference—$7000 to $10,000, for example—the negotiation could take longer, with some interesting twists and turns.

Whether it's an easy or a tough negotiation, never stop promoting yourself. Don't sell yourself short and don't be too willing to compromise. No matter how pressured you are to make a decision, never lose sight of your powerful selling points. Don't hesitate to spell out your qualifications clearly so employers know exactly what you can do. The more confidence you exude, the stronger your case. Salary negotiation will be a lot easier once you firmly establish your value.

Proceed cautiously if you're asking for a lot more than the employer is willing to pay. Be steadfast and confident, but, at the same time, don't price yourself out of a job. Flexibility is the name of the negotiating game. It's a lot easier justifying a bigger salary if you already have medical benefits and life insurance, for example. Employers often fail to realize older workers are not as costly as younger ones because many don't require the standard benefits package.

Advice: If the salary figure is unacceptable, consider negotiating alternative work conditions, such as taking a consulting contract or making a part-time arrangement. Another option is accepting a lower salary with the condition that your salary will be raised a set percentage after you've proven yourself in 6 months. Or take a lower salary until an agreed-upon sales or productivity goal is met. You may also have some creative suggestions of your own. The point is you have more leverage than you realize.

It's a whole new job game with revised rules. Don't hesitate to impress employers with your flexibility. If you happen to latch onto a long-term job, excellent. If not, you'll find something else. But, if you have to compromise, do so sparingly.

Make it clear you'll compromise—to a point. Yes, you want the job, but you're not going to work for an insulting salary—not at your level. You've got your pride, dignity, and self-esteem, and that's ultimately more important than a paycheck. Exhibit that point and you'll gain big points on the respect ladder.

LAST-DITCH EFFORT: "WE'LL HAVE TO THINK ABOUT IT"

Don't get bent out of shape if you don't arrive at a happy figure in one sitting. As much as you'd love to have wrapped it up, the employer may pull one last-ditch tactic and say, "We understand where you're coming from, Mr. Clinton, but since you're asking for more than we planned to pay, I'd like to think it over for a couple of days."

If the employer has partners or associates, you may get this one: "Since you're asking for 35 percent more than we planned on paying, I'd like to discuss this with my colleagues to find a solution we can all live with."

Don't let it throw you. Show regret, concern, or angst and they've got you. Be confident, controlled, and always the consummate professional and you'll remain in the driver's seat. Whatever happens, don't let it phase you. Say something understanding and professional like, "I can understand that, Mr. Tightwad. Maybe we could speak over the next couple of days. I look forward to picking up the ball again. I'm sure we can arrive at a harmonious figure."

Fact is Mr. Tightwad doesn't have to consult anyone or ask anyone's permission. He knew exactly what he could spend before he met with you. All he's doing is using a stall tactic to make you nervous. He's hoping you'll blow your cool thinking about other candidates who might be offered *the* job. Maybe you'll get so uptight, you'll grab the phone and take the job at the salary offered. Not on your life! A little paranoia is normal, but don't let it sabotage you. As tough as it sounds, hang in there for a couple of days. I'm betting Tightwad calls you before you call him. Reminder: He wants you.

Another popular scare tactic is tossing budgetary restraints in your face. "Since you're asking for far more than we budgeted for the position, I'd like to discuss this with my controller to see if the salary you're asking for is financially feasible. We've carefully budgeted all our key expenses for the next 12 months."

Baloney. It sounds great, but it's a lot of hot air. Don't believe a word of it. They're trying to make you believe the old corporate line that budgets are cast in stone.

As soon as you hear them say "budget," you know they're grasping at straws. Yes, most smart companies have budgets. And yes, they do their damnedest to stick to them. Yet every day budgets are bent, stretched, and sometimes abandoned. Typically, it's for a critical expenditure. When a highly qualified person comes along demanding more than the allotted pay for that function, employers do some bottom-line rationalizing. "So it's $10,000 over budget. Look what we're getting. Sure we could get someone cheaper. But she won't have the experience of this seasoned professional." Ten minutes of logical thinking leads to an inevitable conclusion: "The bottom line could be conservatively fattened by at least 20 percent by hiring this capable person. Call Ms. Aristotle and ask her when she can start." Done deal.

Do you feel better now that you know what went on behind the scenes?

FIVE ALL-PURPOSE COMMANDMENTS

Here are five all-purpose commandments for smart salary negotiation:

1. Know what you're worth. Check out the market carefully so you're cutting the best deal.
2. Don't bring up salary until a job offer is made.
3. Don't be afraid to build a strong case for yourself. Employers respect and admire candidates who are unafraid to sell themselves. Ninety percent of salary negotiation is convincing employers you're indispensable.
4. Be patient. Negotiations can take a few days.
5. Negotiate in a friendly manner. Don't be evasive, belligerent, or confrontational. Remember, the employer has decided to hire you and doesn't want to go through the timely and expensive chore of screening other applicants.

Next, let's wrap it up and get the deal in writing.

CEMENT THE DEAL AND GET IT IN WRITING

Congratulations! It was a hard-fought battle, but you did it. You've got the job and a place to hang out for a while. Before you check out your new office and meet the crew, some important details have to be ironed out. First, discuss all the nitty-gritty details of your job with your new boss. Second, sum it up in writing.

PUT IT ALL ON THE TABLE

You've been playing the job game a long time. You've probably witnessed plenty of misunderstandings and unmet promises between employers and employees. "Well, I thought I was going to be doing this" is a common lament. Or you were under the impression the job entailed less than 5 percent travel time. Five months later, you discover 20 percent of your time is spent on the road. And you're pretty unhappy because you feel trapped. Wires can easily be crossed. Avoid trouble by going over all the crucial details of your job before you start. Make no assumptions and get answers to all the following questions:

1. What are my responsibilities?
2. Where will I be working? A private office? Cubicle? Behind the garage?
3. Who are the people I will be working with?
4. To whom will I report?
5. What are my hours?

6. What is my salary, commission on new accounts, incentive pay, and so on?

7. How much travel will I be doing?

8. What are the benefits (medical and life insurance, vacations) and perks (car, expense account)?

9. What are my promotional opportunities? When will I be reviewed?

Once everything is on the table, summarize the key points of your discussion in a letter of agreement between you and your employer. Is it necessary? you ask. Absolutely! At your level, you ought to be the consummate professional right down to the last detail. The letter not only outlines your responsibilities, it also contains a what-if scenario. What happens if it doesn't work out and your services are no longer needed? Do you shake hands, clear your desk, and split? Not on your life. Spell out those what-if scenarios in a letter.

For example, if the employer deems your services unacceptable for whatever reason, you'll be given at least 2 weeks' notice and, depending upon how long you've worked there, be provided with appropriate severance pay. Many employers may not go for this fine point, but you're foolish not to try.

A POLITE BUT FIRM AGREEMENT

Don't think you're being a picayune nitpicker either. You're simply protecting yourself. If you don't do so, who will? The letter achieves the following:

1. If there is disagreement over responsibilities or terms of employment, the letter can straighten it out quickly, avoiding awkward confrontations.

2. If there is a merger or takeover, you can present the letter to your new bosses. It's no guarantee you won't be booted into the street. But you never know; they may be impressed and ask you to stick around.

3. If you're unlawfully fired because of age discrimination, the letter may help you in court. It's evidence: proof, an explanation of

your employment relationship. But remember it's not a binding legal document that's going to help you win a million-dollar settlement. Since each state has its own employment laws, there's no predicting how such a document would be interpreted.

Think of it all as a polite but firm agreement between you and the employer. Use the letter on the following page as a model.

Keep it short and sweet. Remember, you may have to modify certain paragraphs, especially the severance section. A shrewd employer may just agree to the 2 weeks' notice part and not promise to pay you anything. Play it by ear.

After the letter is signed and dated by both parties, keep the original and give a copy to your boss. It wouldn't be a bad idea to send another copy to your lawyer to keep on file. You never know when it may come in handy.

The smart job hunter is ready for anything. Chances are you'll never have to look at this letter again. But you never know.

Even though you're soon to be working again, the game isn't over. In the next chapter you'll find out what's left to do.

January 23, 19XX

Mr. Stanley Spider
Access Software, Inc.
224 Arlington Terrace
Virginia Beach, FL XXXXX

Dear Mr. Spider:

This letter summarizes the employment agreement between Roger Ouchright and Access Software.

I am to begin working at Access on Monday, 9 a.m., as marketing manager of the Northeast Region. Reporting to me will be four assistant managers who'll monitor accounts on a daily basis. I'm to report to Stanley Spider, president.

My primary function is to build sales in the Northeast Region through creative sales and marketing tools. I'm expected to develop new marketing campaigns which will first be approved by Mr. Spider. Once approval and budgets are set, I'm responsible for implementation and making them work. Approximately 10 percent of my time will be spent visiting regional offices and developing new accounts.

My yearly salary is $75,000, plus a 10 percent commission on every new account I bring in. I'm to be reviewed every 6 months. If, after a year, my campaigns boost sales at least 20 percent, my salary will be increased by a minimum of 12 percent. I'm entitled to 2 weeks' vacation in my first year of employment; after that, vacation time increases to 3 weeks.

If, for any reason, I'm terminated because I fail to meet my job goals, I will be given at least 2 weeks' notice plus 3 weeks' pay for every year I worked at the company.

Sincerely,

Roger Ouchright (Date)

Stanley Spider (Date)

DON'T GET TOO COMFORTABLE— THE WAR AIN'T OVER

If you try, you can do almost anything you want.
R. DAVID THOMAS
Founder of Wendy's

Now that life is calmer, I can almost guess what you're thinking. It feels great to be joining the working world again. You can dump all the job-hunting rituals—scanning daily want ads, talking to anyone within shouting distance about job leads, and networking yourself into a stupor. The battle is won. You can hang up your flak jacket and helmet and put down your weapons. Relax and enjoy your newfound security.

Stop! Yes, a major burden has been lifted from your shoulders. You did great. But the game isn't over by any stretch of the imagination just because you landed a job. Maybe in the 1960s and 1970s you could have folded up and gotten comfortable and never thought about finding another job. Not in the frenetic 1990s.

For the moment everything feels and looks right. Maybe you think you've found job nirvana. It's possible, but I wouldn't put money on it. It's normal to get excited about starting a job. After all, it's all spanking new—the work, people, and place. You feel like a kid with a new toy. For the first week or so, the toy is your favorite. After that, it's on to bigger and better ones.

Naturally, your interest level will be longer than a child's. But the point is important. You may lose interest after 6 months or a year. Maybe the job wasn't what you expected. The people weren't high-energy motivators who turned you on. Or maybe it was just the opposite. Unknowingly, you walked into a cutthroat kill-or-be-killed fast-track company whose pace could be likened to the Indianapolis 500. Every day is like riding on an out-of-control roller coaster and you can't wait to climb out. Or your boss, who seemed perfectly normal when you met her, turned into a screaming virago who ought to be caged and exiled to a deserted island.

Alternatively, you may love your new job, but the company suddenly experiences rough waters and is close to capsizing. Whether the cause is incompetent management, a pending merger, or bankruptcy, it looks like you'll have to grab your life jacket and bail out. The final scenario is you may wind up finishing out your career there.

I'm not being negative or pessimistic, just cautious and pragmatic. I urge you to adopt the same attitude. Look at the facts. What is better evidence than the business world of the past decade? I don't have to tell you what's happened. You lived it. And it wasn't pleasant. The days of blindly trusting an organization are over. Hopefully, you've learned that the only person you can trust is yourself. Again, I'll scream it from the rafters: There's no such thing as job certainty. Lifetime employment is a myth. Today, you're happily employed. But only God knows what tomorrow will bring. And don't expect road signs warning of bumps and potholes in the distance. You must anticipate them.

Advice: Don't get too comfortable. Do the best work you can, yet have your bags packed so you can split if things turn bad.

TAKE AN ORGANIZATIONAL READING

Once you get past the "Welcome aboard, we're all one big happy family, let's work together as a team to create something special" stuff and all the rah-rah slogans many companies enjoy shoveling at new staffers, get down to brass tacks and check out the place—from the loading dock to the executive suite.

Keep your antenna up at all times and be street-smart. Waste no time creating alliances. Build a wall of support by making friends in the right places. Learn how the political structure works and identify the power brokers. These are the folks you ought to befriend and, if nothing else, respect. Protect yourself by having allies at all organizational levels. Uppermost, plug into the company grapevine so you find out information as it's happening, rather than after the fact. That way, you'll always be current.

I'm a great believer in backscratching—"You scratch my back and I'll scratch yours." As Michael Mercer points out in *How Winners Do It: High-Impact Skills for Your Career Success*, it's one of the oldest techniques, virtually assuring win-win outcomes. Favors must be returned. True power brokers can be likened to loan sharks. Unselfishly, they go out of their way to help everyone, especially those in influential positions. At the right moment, they knock on doors asking for payback—plus interest.

The more people owing you favors, the stronger your position. Only a fool doesn't ask for payback. "Remember when I helped you meet that deadline last month, Hortense? Well, I need you to run interference and help me persuade Larry to okay that budget request on my new project." What do you think her answer will be? A rhetorical question for sure.

BE VISIBLE

Even though it's great building plenty of support at all levels, it's also important to be visible and distinguish yourself early in the game. Companies want to see a "take charge" attitude. If you convey the impression you're ready and willing to put your heart and soul into your work, even if you have to throw yourself in front of a speeding freight train, you've earned star-studded points. It's the equivalent of capturing Boardwalk and Park Place in a Monopoly game. You've won respect and power at the same time, giving you strategic leverage.

Trust earns you the privilege of schmoozing with secretaries and back-office folks during coffee breaks and sipping martinis with their bosses after working hours.

KEEP YOUR NETWORK ALIVE

Outside of work, keep in touch with your network. Sadly, this is the time it's often neglected. Once you're comfortably employed, don't mistakenly let down your guard. The best time to beef up your network is when you're safe (temporarily at least) and pulling down a steady paycheck. Frequent telephone conversations, lunches, or afterwork drinks with industry contacts could reveal incredible leads. Keep the networking lines open 24 hours a day and you may stumble on an even better job. What then? It's your decision. Weigh your options and go with your gut. One of the thrills of piloting a career is taking calculated risks.

Sure your new boss wouldn't be very happy if you jumped ship only a month after you started. But then again, what would she do in the same situation?

The irony is it's amazing how job offers suddenly surface once you're employed. Where were they when you needed them 3 months ago? It's not worth having a temper tantrum over it. The good news is you're in the power seat. You can evaluate potential job offers from a position of strength. You can be totally objective and pick the cream of the crop. Don't tell me it's not an incredible feeling. Uppermost, you've got the luxury of time to map a contingency plan.

ALWAYS HAVE ONE FOOT OUT THE DOOR

Give yourself 3 months to settle in at your new employer. Then, it's time to start working out a contingency plan.

Why so soon? Like I said, you don't know what tomorrow may bring. You'd be surprised how fast things can turn. The sooner you start making alternative plans, the better you'll feel. I guarantee you'll sleep better—not to mention, do a better job. Having other irons in the fire gives you a wonderful feeling of control. Even if you never exercise these plans, it's nice to know they're in place and ready to activate on a moment's notice. The more elaborate they are, the better. They could identify several potential employers or maybe a business you've been thinking about starting for years. There are no rules or restrictions. You can design the plan any way you like, as long as it's action-oriented and puts you back in the game so you don't skip a beat.

And don't just think and talk it. Put everything down on paper so it's real and you can expand upon it.

The message is to keep on moving. As the saying goes, "Always be a moving target." Whatever you do, don't get so comfortable you're lulled into a false sense of security. Be careful, it happens everyday. Hardly a few months into the job, you may swear you've found a permanent home. You say to yourself, "Wow, this is like the old days." As soon as that occurs, you've taken a step backward.

You've been bought. You think you've found the perfect job. Your coworkers are great and your boss has promised you the world. You've gone out for drinks with him, and you and your spouse have been invited to his house for dinner.

All well and good. It's great being appreciated, but don't make the mistake of believing every promise made. Maybe the promises were true for the moment, but who can predict the future? If the business suffers one bad quarter, a disastrous season, or a recession, all bets are off. Remember, this is business, a game with no rules. Like they say, if it seems too good to be true, it probably is. Be appreciative, do your best work, but remain cynical. If you want to come out ahead, keep your eyes on the players.

Years ago, I learned to think of myself as a kind of traveling salesman whose bags are always packed. It's a healthy survival attitude that keeps you on your toes, ready to move on down that career highway.

STAY CURRENT

Finally, consider taking some courses at a local college or university. Who knows? You may get a second wind and decide to enroll in a degree program. It's happening more and more. Thankfully, the higher-learning environment has changed. There are many more learning options; more important, the nation's college population is no longer solely 18- to 21-year-olds. Today, almost half of college students are over age 24 and more than 63,000 are over 65. It's not like the old days when "mature" students were intimidated by a sea of young faces. Expect to find plenty of graying heads in the crowd.

More people are returning to school late in life for all kinds of reasons. Some do it for career purposes, such as to stay current with their industry. Others do so to fill gaps in their education, and still others return out of curiosity. Think about how great it could be to take any course you want without the pressure of piling up credits for graduation. That's right—doing it for sheer pleasure. It's no wonder people in their fifties and sixties discover talents they never knew they had. A course in writing, painting, sculpture, filmmaking, or computer programming opens a trap door in your mind. And you may say to yourself, "Why didn't I do this earlier?" Whatever the reason, don't beat yourself up over it. Be thankful you discovered a newfound passion.

It doesn't really matter where a course or two leads. Whatever you take and whatever your motives, I guarantee you'll profit from the experience. Like being primed and ready to jump on new opportunities or bail out of your job when things get rough, feeding the brain with new information is as important as fueling your body with food. It's yet another thing to do to keep in shape. As I said, the battle is won, but the war ain't over.

Let's start to wind down with some homespun philosophy.

CHAPTER
TWENTY-THREE

SO YOU WANT TO
BE RICH!

Don't be trapped by old concepts.
Invasion of the Body Snatchers
(1978)

No profit grows where is no pleasure taken.
WILLIAM SHAKESPEARE (1564–1616)

Rumor has it the older you get, the smarter you get. That's the way it ought to be. But that's not always the way the world works. When I was a naive kid who thought he had all the answers, I swore being rich translated to a fat bank account. What else would you expect from someone who grew up in the hinterlands of Brooklyn? I believed that until the sky opened up in my mid-thirties. I looked around at the people I knew well and began to put the pieces together.

Most of my friends were building careers at supersonic speed, working outlandish hours and buying all the gadgets they could get their hands on. They were whirling dervishes who never shut down. The salaries, cars, and lavish lifestyles were their scorecards. They were adults playing a real-world game of Monopoly—the wealthiest person had the most stuff. But none of my friends were really rich, because they didn't truly love what they did. Their jobs were a means to an end, rather than an end in and of itself. I'll wager they'll keep at it until they burn out or have coronaries, whichever comes first.

Then I thought about my father, who died at the age of 60, when I was 22. He was a self-made man who grew up in abject poverty in one of the toughest sections of Brooklyn. To his family, he was a hero, a trailblazer, the proud product of peasant East European immigrants who couldn't speak a stitch of English but went on to make something of himself. Not only did he graduate college; he did it on a full-tuition scholarship while holding down a part-time job that helped support his family. Capturing a degree in dentistry was his ticket to success and opened up a new world he couldn't wait to taste.

Despite all that, my father never saw himself as rich. He lived a modest, unassuming lifestyle with one car and a small house, but no boat, plane, chauffeur, or live-in maid. He walked to work and ate at the same diner 5 days a week, a place where he knew everyone from short-order cooks to busboys on a first-name basis.

The mistake my father made was comparing himself with others, who he felt had done much better. Many of his peers drove better cars, lived in bigger homes, and took lavish vacations.

As smart as he was, he never realized his arithmetic was bad. He was tallying the wrong things. He was doing exactly what my friends are doing—keeping score in a conventional way. He seldom thought about where he came from, what he had accomplished, and uppermost, what he had. At the top of the heap, he loved his work. And that's where he invested most of his energy and time. He couldn't wait to get to work in the morning. It didn't bother him that most of his patients were petrified of spending an hour in his chair. The magic ritual he performed daily was allaying his patients' fears.

Looking back, I see a man who had it all together. He made it. He was rich. The moral of this story is there is no such thing as a bad job—*if you love what you do*. Get your hands around that one and you'll understand the secret of wealth and power, maybe even the meaning of life itself. In *Sharkproof*, supersalesman Harvey Mackay says being rich is a state of mind. He's right. What's more, it's relative.

ARE YOU SURE YOU WANT TO REACH THE WHITE HOUSE?

Blame it on Madison Avenue or dumb TV shows like *Lifestyles of the Rich and Famous*. The problem is we apply the same success standards to everyone. Naively, we assume everyone shares the same drives and ambitions. Would you like to be President of the United States, run a *Fortune* 500 company, or become a powerful attorney? You say no to all three. What about becoming an entrepreneur and launching the next Microsoft, Wendy's, or Home Depot? No, again. Don't despair, it's perfectly okay. Maybe you'd like to do something more modest like repair furniture, design perfume bottles, be a rubberband purveyor, or run a small country inn. None of these turn me on, but plenty of people out there are working in such careers and having the time of their lives.

The key is to *do what you love*. Don't beat yourself up if your goals are modest and you don't have the drive, energy, or metabolism to climb mountains. The fantasy perpetuated on the tube is that success is set aside for the chosen, the workaholics, fast-trackers, the superambitious go-getters who've sacrificed their souls for their careers. The ostentatious exhibitionists on TV shows like *Lifestyles* are the exception, not the rule. They account for a minuscule fraction of the population. And, I daresay, if most people enjoyed that kind of wealth, they'd be far more discreet about it.

Plenty of folks lead quiet, modest lives and aren't working 60-hour weeks. They're driving Fords and Chevys, leaving work at 5 p.m., and eating dinner with their families every night of the week. Maybe they're doing volunteer work every Monday night and bowling with their friends on Wednesdays. Are these regular folks successful? If they love their jobs and lifestyles, you bet they are. What about you?

THE SUCCESS TEST

How do you stack up? Are you successful or are you still waiting for your proverbial horse to cross the finish line? Here's a quick test that will give you the answer. It's painless, and it takes only a minute. Answer these three questions:

1. Do you love your work?
2. Do you earn enough to maintain a comfortable lifestyle meeting your needs?
3. What changes, if any, would you make to improve your life?

If you answered the first two questions with a yes and the third with a none, you're rich. If you enjoy good health in the bargain, you're ahead of the pack. If you answered with a qualifier such as maybe or an outright no, what would you do to improve the situation? Mind you, "comfortable lifestyle meeting your needs" is subject to interpretation. If you're the Duke of Windsor, comfortable may mean a couple of castles, estates, a herd of racing horses, and a small army of servants for starters. Realistically, how many homes does anyone actually need? Seriously, most of us are perfectly content with a lot less than we think.

I hope you don't think my quickie test too simple. Why must everything be complicated? I strongly believe the greatest insights are right under our noses. All we have to do is open our eyes and look for them.

ARE YOU READY FOR THE MEANING OF LIFE?

When you think about it, making a wad of money is a pretty ridiculous mission in life. Not only is it shallow and empty, it's also meaningless. Once you have wealth, what then? You're faced with the real mission in life: finding something that offers both meaning and fulfillment. It really doesn't matter what it is. Why is it so many disillusioned stockbrokers, attorneys, physicians, and corporate executives chuck high-profile careers to become teachers? The answer is mission and meaning, which are indelibly intertwined.

Maybe I'm a hopeless Puritan at heart, but I advocate there is virtue in good work.

Understanding and believing this simple concept is the first step; living it is the ultimate accomplishment. The best part is that finding this utopia removes an enormous pressure off your shoulders, making life a lot more fun.

The meaning of life? Again, it's working at something you love until you're unable to work. If you agree with me, why on earth would you even consider retiring? I'll dispel any doubts you have in the final chapter.

RETIRE? ARE YOU KIDDING!

The person who has lived the most is not the one with the most years, but the one with the richest experiences.   JEAN JACQUES ROUSSEAU
Emile (1762)

Ever wonder why people retire? Take it from me, it's usually for the wrong reasons. The only valid time to stop working is when you have no reason to get up in the morning. If I made any sense in the prior chapter, you'll never see that day. Like the myth that says success and money are intimately intertwined, another one says that when you get to be 65 you ought to think about hanging up your guns and retiring. It's utter dribble. If you love what you do, why on earth would you think about retiring? If you're approaching 75 or 80, maybe you'll lighten your load and put in fewer hours, but *retire?* Never. Don't believe those insulting brokerage house ads that show graying men and women out fishing in some pastoral setting, perpetually smiling in retirement euphoria. Yes, it looks inviting, but try fishing and golfing 12 months a year. I guarantee you'll go out of your mind.

RETIREMENT: A POST-WORLD WAR II PHENOMENON

Let's straighten out this retirement myth once and for all. Our generation grew up thinking retirement was a great thing. We were raised to believe life parallels those nauseating family sitcoms of the late 1950s and 1960s. According to them, you sow your oats, get a job, marry, raise a family, and retire. Boy, life was depicted as real simple back then. But now you know different. For many, the idea of one job, one spouse, and one family is all baloney! And retirement? Practically speaking, many baby boomers who think they'd like to retire simply can't afford to stop working.

Don't for a minute assume retirement is a privilege of age and wealth that dates back centuries. Actually, it's a post-World War II phenomenon, a product of the New Deal's Social Security Administration. In fact, mandatory retirement was deemed illegal in the late 1980s because it violated age discrimination statutes and the Employee Retirement Income Security Act (ERISA). ERISA was created in 1974 to protect retirement funds and oversee the people who administer them.

What's more, social security benefits can no longer meet most of our retirement needs. Government pundits say the Social Security Administration is running out of money. In 1984, just up to half of benefits were taxable; a decade later, the tax rate jumped to over 85 percent. The more you make, the more the government takes. In 1945, there were approximately 42 workers for every beneficiary, according to the Social Security Administration. In 1950, the number dropped to 16.5; by 1994, it tumbled to 3.2; and by the year 2010, it's projected to be 2.9 workers for every beneficiary.

We grew up thinking social security benefits would take care of us in our retirement years. That's no longer the case. With people living longer, the number of retirees eligible for social security will continue to grow while the worker base needed to support them will not keep pace. Twenty-first-century pragmatism has replaced New Deal idealism.

GET OVER THE FANTASY

Beyond financial realities, the idea of retirement has been elevated to an unrealistic fantasy in most people's minds. That's not to say there aren't plenty of men and women who long for the day they can quit their jobs and do things they've dreamed about all their lives. But they're the exception, not the rule. Most people retire either because they hate their jobs or because they've had enough of the rat race. Sooner or later, though, retirement almost always backfires.

If you doubt me, listen to these true sagas. I bet you never heard of the St. Louis, MO, support group called the Cashed Out Presidents Society (COPS). COPS is a forum through which cashed-out presidents and company founders help one another deal with retirement. According to COPS founder J. W. Kisling, the group started with 6 people in 1985 and now has 30 members who pay dues of $75 a year.

It sounds crazy but these folks, who have a collective net worth of more than half a billion dollars, don't know what to do with themselves now that they've sold their businesses to another company. Imagine not knowing how to enjoy yourself with a few million dollars in the bank? COPS proves my point. It's not about money, but about wanting to continue to do something that keeps you excited 12 hours a day. Why did these entrepreneurs dump the successful companies they built with their own hands? Simple. Like everyone else, they believed the retirement myth. After working long and hard, they figured it was time to enjoy the fruits of their labor. Nice concept, but it doesn't fly. COPS meetings are devoted to helping members jump back into the fray. Most wind up starting or buying another company. COPS founder Kisling sold one and is now running another.

Or take my friend, A. J. Richard, the 86-year-old founder and chairman of the board at P. C. Richard & Son, a $500-million-a-year electronics empire. Five days a week, he's in his office by 7:30 a.m., drinking black coffee and chomping on a Jamaican cigar. When I asked A. J. why he still comes to work, rather than spending his millions, he said, "If I couldn't work, I'd die." Money is not the issue, my friends.

So don't feel sorry for yourself because you have to work. Don't be depressed because some of your retired friends are playing golf when you're shoveling toast and coffee into your mouth so you can make the 7 a.m. train to be at work on time. Take it from me, most of your retired friends aren't happy. You're in better shape than they are. They may have bigger bank accounts, but you're healthier because you're still out there fighting the war. They've checked out, you haven't. The sad part is they regret it.

IF GEORGE FOREMAN CAN DO IT, SO CAN YOU!

So don't cash out. As I said earlier, don't see yourself as washed up and operating at half steam. Let fighter George Foreman be your inspiration. On that historic Saturday night in Las Vegas in November 1994, Foreman, at the age of 45, knocked out opponent

Michael Moorer in the tenth round, making him the oldest professional fighter to win the championship in any weight class. As one
sportswriter put it, "Foreman crossed the line between athlete and
icon." No wonder Foreman has been dubbed "Father Time."
Traditionally, fighters peak in their mid-thirties. By their early forties, they're used up.

Foreman broke the pattern. He quit boxing in 1977, but not
because his career was over. After a 45-2 record, including 42
knockouts, he figured it was time for a career change and became a
streetcorner preacher. But when he needed money to support his
parish, he returned to the ring. The rest is history. At a portly 250
pounds, Foreman is a force not to be reckoned with. It's no wonder
Madison Avenue marketing consultants are pounding on his door
begging him to endorse a slew of products for the 40-plus generation. If Foreman has what it takes—in his forties—to knock out a
26-year-old, what makes you think he can't do it again at 50? If that
doesn't teach Generation X a lesson, I don't know what will.

If Foreman can do the impossible—break stereotypes and blow
conventional thinking to smithereens—so can you. He saw no limits
or barriers and said the hell with this age stuff. I'm tough and
strong, and *so what if I'm 45?* I'm going to get in the ring and pound
that kid into the tarp. He did just that.

You ought to adopt the same attitude. So what if you're 50, 55,
60, or 80? You're only defeated if you think you are.

THERE IS NO SECOND ACT

As I wind down, my important message is that people were meant to
be busy and do meaningful work. Everyone must define meaningful
in his or her own way. This sounds preachy, but the simple truth is
work is our salvation. We define ourselves by what we do. Stop
working and suddenly we're lost, adrift in perilous seas without a
compass. Talk to people who have tried retirement and you'll get
powerful insights into the true value of work. Beyond psychological
and financial rewards, work gives purpose and structure to our lives.

Practically speaking, the best defense against obsolescence is
work. As marketing gurus Al Ries and Jack Trout said in *Horse
Sense,* "There is no second act." This is it. The spotlight is on you;
the audience is waiting with baited breath. Take your cues and give

it the performance of your life. I mean the very best. Continue to pour your heart and soul into whatever it is you enjoy doing. Keep at it until the very end and chances are good you'll go out smiling.

What more could anyone ask for?

INFORMATION SOURCES

To make your life easier, here's a potpourri of solid information sources.

COMPANY SOURCES

The Hoover group of handbooks is available in most libraries. For information, write to The Reference Press, Inc., 6448 Highway 290 E., Suite E-104, Austin, TX 78723; (512) 454-7778.

- *Hoover's Masterlist of Major U.S. Companies* is updated yearly and offers information on more than 6000 companies.
- *Computer Industry Almanac* covers more than 2500 computer companies.
- *Hoover's Handbook of Emerging Companies* offers one-page snapshots of high-profile leaders plus a look at smaller companies with great potential.

Planning/Communications (River Forest, IL 60305; 708-366-5200) publishes two useful resources by Daniel Lauber. Both can be found in the career sections of major book chains.

- *Professional Private Sector Job Finder* lists jobs by industry grouping—apparel and accessories, architecture, entertainment, and so on.
- *Non-Profits Job Finder* breaks out nonprofit jobs by sector, such as agriculture, education, and health.

Practically all of Dun & Bradstreet's reference books are available in libraries. For information, write to Dun & Bradstreet

Information Services Products, One Diamond Road, Murray Hill, NJ 07974-0027; (800) 526-0651.

- *Million Dollar Directory*, a five-volume series, offers information on 160,000 mid-size companies, more than 90 percent of which are privately held. Listings include company name, subsidiaries, address, phone number, principal officers, number of employees, sales volume, and more.
- *Dun's Regional Business Directory* is a three-volume set with facts and figures on 20,000 public and private regional businesses.
- *Dun's Employment Opportunities Directory/The Career Guide* is an all-in-one directory detailing hiring practices and employment opportunities at 5000 U.S. companies. It lists short corporate histories, promising employment areas, education requirements, addresses, phone numbers, and people to contact for information.

CorpTech, located in Woburn, MA 01801, focuses on current and emerging technologies. For information, call (800) 333-8036.

- *The CorpTech Directory*, updated yearly, is a reliable source offering capsulized pictures of the high-tech arena. It lists over 35,000 U.S. public and private technology companies, plus rapidly growing firms with fewer than 100 employees.
- *The Technology Industry Growth Forecaster* is a four-page monthly newsletter containing timely information on hot private companies, emerging technologies, and promising locations.

Maybe you didn't know it, but the U.S. government publishes a truckload of free information. (In actuality, your taxes pay for it.) The two best sources are the Commerce Department and the Department of Labor.

- The Commerce Department publishes a raft of material on the state of U.S. industry. Most publications include 5-year projections. Its yearly *U.S. Industrial Outlook* is an information-rich tome covering business forecasts of more than 350 industries. Each section offers a 3- to 10-page sketch of the industry. For information, write U.S. Department of Commerce, Office of Business Analysis, 14th and Constitution Ave. NW, Room 4885, Washington, DC 20230.

- The Department of Labor's Bureau of Labor Statistics (BLS) publishes monthly labor reports for the nation in addition to regional reports. For information on specific careers (job descriptions, qualifications, salaries, outlook, and where to get information), look at BLS's recent edition of the *Occupational Outlook Handbook*. Most libraries carry at least one copy.

- The BLS also publishes the *Occupational Outlook Quarterly*, which provides industry forecasts and job market projections until 2005. If you can't find the publication at your library, consider subscribing to it. Write the Superintendent of Documents, U.S. Government Printing Office, Washington, DC 20402. Or contact the U.S. Department of Labor, Bureau of Labor Statistics, Publications Sales Office, Box 2145, Chicago, IL 60690.

- The BLS has eight regional offices scattered throughout the United States. It pays to call the one nearest you to be put on its mailing list. This will put you on top of your state's job market. While it's not a current information source, the BLS is great for statistical and trend data. Below are the BLS regional offices:

Boston   1 Congress St., 10th Floor, Boston, MA 02114

New York   201 Farrier St., Room 808, New York, NY 10014

Philadelphia   P.O. Box 13309, Philadelphia, PA 19101

Atlanta   1371 Peachtree St. NE, Atlanta, GA 30367

Chicago   Federal Office Building, 130 South Dearborn St., 9th Floor, Chicago, IL 60604

Dallas   Federal Building, 525 Grifin St., Room 221, Dallas, TX 75202

Kansas City   911 Walnut St., Kansas City, MO 64106

San Francisco   71 Stevenson St., P.O. Box 193766, San Francisco, CA 94119

BONING UP ON NONPROFITS

Interested in learning about nonprofits—fund raising, grant writing, and other career possibilities? Below are 25 colleges and universities offering programs. Call one near you for a catalog.

CALIFORNIA

University of California/San
  Francisco
Carroll L. Estes
Chairman, Department of Social
  and Behavioral Science
Director, Institute for Health and
  Aging
Room N-631Y, Box 0612
San Francisco, CA 94143-0610
(415) 476-1253

University of San Francisco
Michael O'Neill
Director, Institute for Nonprofit
  Organization Management
College of Professional Studies
Ignatian Heights
San Francisco, CA 94117-1080
(415) 666-6867

COLORADO

Regis University
Roger Kahn, Director
Center for Nonprofit Leadership
3539 West 50th Parkway
Denver, CO 80221
(303) 458-4100

CONNECTICUT

Yale University
Bradford Gray
Executive Director, Program on
  Nonprofit Organizations
88 Trumbull St.
New Haven, CT 06520-0154
(203) 432-2124

ILLINOIS

Northwestern University
Center for Urban Affairs and Policy
  Research
Burton Weisbrod, Director
John Evans, Professor of
  Economics
2040 Sheridan Road
Evanston, IL 60208-4100
(608) 223-9574

INDIANA

Indiana University/Purdue
  University at Indianapolis
Robert L. Payton
Director and Professor of
  Philanthropic Studies
Center on Philanthropy
550 West North St., Suite 301
Indianapolis, IN 46202-3162
(317) 274-4200

LONDON

Centre for Voluntary Organization
David Billis
Department of Social Science and
  Administration
The London School of Economics
  and Political Administration
Houghton St.
London, WC2A 2AE England
(01) 405-7686
(71) 242-0392

MARYLAND

Johns Hopkins University
Lester M. Salamon
Director, Institute for Policy
  Studies
Shriver Hall
Baltimore, MD 21218
(410) 516-7174

MASSACHUSETTS

Boston College
Paul G. Schervish
Director, Social Welfare Research
  Institute
515 McGuinn Hall, Room 516
Chestnut Hill, MA 02167
(617) 552-3199

Tufts University
Robert Hollister
Director, Lincoln Filene Center for
  Citizenship and Public Affairs
Medford, MA 02155
(617) 381-3656

MINNESOTA

University of St. Thomas
Ricky Littlefield
Director, Nonprofit and Public
  Management
Mail #4635, 2115 Summit Ave.
St. Paul, MN 55105
(612) 647-5538

MISSOURI

University of Missouri/Kansas City
Robert D. Herman
Professor, Cookingham Institute
Program on Nonprofit and Public
  Service Leadership
Room 212 Bloch, 51-10 Charity
Kansas City, MO 64110
(816) 235-2338

NEW JERSEY

Seton Hall University
Naomi Wish, Director, Center for
  Public Service
Duffy Hall, Room 62
South Orange, NJ 07079-2691
(201) 761-9788

NEW YORK

Graduate School and University
  Center
City University of New York
Kathleen D. McCarthy
Director, Center for the Study of
  Philanthropy
33 West 42nd St., Room 1512
New York, NY 10036
(212) 642-2130

New School for Social Research
John Palmer Smith, Associate
  Professor and Chairman
66 Fifth Ave.
New York, NY 10011
(212) 229-5434

New York Law School
Harvey P. Dale
Director, Program on Philanthropy
  and Law
110 West 3rd St., 2nd Floor
New York, NY 10012
(212) 998-6161

New York University
Laura Landy
Director, Center for
  Entrepreneurial Studies
Leonard N. Stern School of
  Business
90 Trinity Place
New York, NY 10006-1594
(212) 285-6150

Rockefeller Archive Center
Darwin H. Stappleton, Director
15 Dayton Ave.
North Tarrytown, NY 10591
(914) 631-4505

NORTH CAROLINA

Duke University
Charles Clotfelter
Director for the Study of
  Philanthropy and Volunteerism
Institute of Policy Sciences and
  Public Affairs
4875 Duke Station
Durham, NC 27706
(919) 684-2672

OHIO

Case Western Reserve University
Dennis Young
Director, Mandel Center for
  Nonprofit Organizations
11235 Bellflower Road, Suite 110
Cleveland, OH 44106-7164
(216) 368-2106

PENNSYLVANIA

University of Pennsylvania
Ira Harkavy
Director, Penn Program for Public
  Service
307-B College Hall
Philadelphia, PA 19104-3325
(215) 898-5351

TEXAS

Texas Christian University
William Ray
Director, Program on Nonprofit
  Organizations
Graduate Studies and Research
P.O. Box 32890
Fort Worth, TX 76129
(817) 921-7472

VIRGINIA

Virginia Polytechnic Institute and
  State University
Oscar M. Williams
Director, Center for Volunteer
  Development
Virginia Cooperative Extension
  Service
Donaldson, Brown, CEC CVD
  Suite
Blacksburg, VA 24061
(703) 231-7966

WASHINGTON, DC

National Center for Nonprofit
  Boards
Nancy Axelrod, Executive Director
1225 19th St. NW, Suite 340
Washington, DC 20036
(202) 452-6262

Union Institute
Mark Rosenman
Director for Public Policy
1731 Connecticut Ave. NW, Suite
  300
Washington, DC 20009-1146
(202) 667-1313

NETWORKING AND JOB LEADS

Below are the addresses of each of the 22 chapters of Forty Plus in the United States.

CALIFORNIA

Forty Plus of Northern California
7440 Lockheed St.
Oakland, CA 94603

Forty Plus of Northern California
1150 N. First, #201
San Jose, CA 95110

Forty Plus of Southern California
23172 Plaza Pt. Dr.
Laguna Hills, CA 92653

Forty Plus of Southern California
8845 University Center Lane
San Diego, CA 92122

COLORADO

Forty Plus of Colorado
3842 S. Mason St.
Ft. Collins, CO 80526

Forty Plus of Colorado
2555 Airport Road
Colorado Springs, CO 80910

Forty Plus of Colorado
800 W. Alameda Ave.
Lakewood, CO 80026

HAWAII

Forty Plus of Hawaii
126 Queen St. #227
Honolulu, HI 96813

MINNESOTA

Forty Plus of Minnesota
14870 Granada #315
St. Paul, MN 55124

NEW YORK

Forty Plus of Buffalo
701 Seneca St.
Buffalo, NY 14210

Forty Plus of New York
15 Park Row
New York, NY 10038

OHIO

Forty Plus of Central Ohio
1100 King Ave.
Columbus, OH 43212

PENNSYLVANIA

Forty Plus of Philadelphia
1218 Chestnut St.
Philadelphia, PA 19107

TEXAS

Forty Plus of Dallas
13140 Coit Road, #300
Dallas, TX 75240

Forty Plus of Houston
2909 Hillcroft, #400
Houston, TX 77057

UTAH

Forty Plus of Utah
5735 S. Redwood Road
Murray, UT 84123

Forty Plus of Utah
480 27th St.
Ogden, UT 84409

Forty Plus of Utah
1550 N. 200 West
Provo, UT 84603

WASHINGTON STATE

Forty Plus of Puget Sound
300 120th Ave. NE, #7
Bellevue, WA 98005

WASHINGTON, D.C.

Forty Plus of Greater Washington
1718 P St. NW
Washington, D.C. 20036

JOB SUPPORT GROUPS

Also investigate local churches, synagogues, YMCAs, and YMHAs. Many offer job counseling, support groups, or both. Check to see if there is a support group clearinghouse near you. It can direct you to local support groups so you can commiserate with fellow job searchers.

THINKING ABOUT RELOCATING?

Entrepreneur magazine ranks the 25 best cities for business opportunities.

LARGE CITIES

1. Atlanta, GA
2. Minneapolis/St. Paul, MN
3. Kansas City, MO
4. Columbus, OH
5. Phoenix, AZ
6. Seattle/Everett, WA
7. Cleveland, OH
8. St. Louis, MO
9. Chicago, IL
10. Tampa Bay/St. Petersburg, FL

MID-SIZE CITIES

1. Amarillo, TX
2. Springfield, IL
3. Canton, OH
4. Springfield, MO
5. Eugene/Springfield, OR
6. Tulsa, OK
7. Salem, OR
8. Knoxville, TN
9. Portland, OR
10. St. Cloud, MN

SMALL CITIES

1. Medford, OR
2. Clarksville, TN/Hopkinsville, KY
3. Eau Claire, WI
4. Columbia, MO
5. Biloxi/Gulfport, MS

INDEX

ABOUT THE AUTHOR

Bob Weinstein is a nationally known and respected journalist and trendwatcher in the career field. He is the author of 10 highly acclaimed books on careers including *Résumés Don't Get Jobs, How to Get a Job in Hard Times, Jobs for the 21st Century,* and the recently published *"I'll Work for Free."*